RETHINKING *Blake's* TEXTUALITY

RETHINKING
Blake's
TEXTUALITY

Molly Anne Rothenberg

UNIVERSITY OF MISSOURI PRESS

COLUMBIA AND LONDON

Copyright © 1993 by
The Curators of the University of Missouri
University of Missouri Press,
Columbia, Missouri 65201
Printed and bound in the
United States of America
All rights reserved
5 4 3 2 1   97 96 95 94 93

Library of Congress Cataloging-in-Publication
Data

Rothenberg, Molly Anne, 1952–
    Rethinking Blake's textuality /
Molly Anne Rothenberg.
    p. cm.
    Includes bibliographical references and
index.
    ISBN 0-8262-0901-7 (alk. paper)
    1. Blake, William, 1757–1827—Criticism,
Textual.   2. Discourse analysis, Literary.
I. Title.
PR4147.R68   1993
821'.7—dc20   93-13510
                                        CIP

Versions of the following sections were published previously and are reprinted by permission: "Epistemological Crisis and the Phenomenalistic Subject," published as "The Provisional Vision of Blake's *Jerusalem*," *Word & Image* 3 (October–December 1987); "Blake's Antimetaphysics and the Subject of Discourse," published as "*Jerusalem*'s 'Forgotten Remembrances': A Blakean Analytic of Narrativity and Ideology," *Genre* 23 (Summer–Fall 1990); and "Re-Citing 'The Bard': Natural Language, Referentiality, and the Possessive Selfhood," published as "Blake Reads 'The Bard': Contextual Displacement and Conditions of Readability in *Jerusalem*," *SEL: Studies in English Literature, 1500–1900* 27 (Summer 1987).

∞™This paper meets the requirements of the American National Standard for Permanence of Paper for Printed Library Materials, Z39.48, 1984.

DESIGNER: KRISTIE LEE
TYPESETTER: CONNELL-ZEKO TYPE & GRAPHICS
PRINTER AND BINDER: THOMSON-SHORE, INC.
TYPEFACES: PALATINO, ZAPF CHANCERY

FOR MY PARENTS

Contents

Acknowledgments ix

Introduction 1

PART ONE
De-Signing Authority

Inspiration Revised 9

Blake's Higher Criticism and the Art of Inspiration 18

Sheep and Goats: Disseminating Authority 27

Bounding Lines 36

Re-Citing "The Bard": Natural Language, Referentiality, and the Possessive Selfhood 48

PART TWO
The Subject of Discourse

The Fall from Hermeneutics and the Rhetoric of Subjectivity 65

Epistemological Crisis and the Phenomenalistic Subject 78

The Typological Subject and the Ratio of Christ 97

Blake's Antimetaphysics and the Subject of Discourse 108

"The Dim Chaos Brightend" and a Possible Politics of Textuality 129

Bibliography 139

Index 155

Acknowledgments

Blake scholars deserve their reputations for generosity to their colleagues. I am grateful to Donald Ault for his detailed and insightful criticism of the manuscript; without his kind assistance, the book would have many more flaws than it does at present. Early in the project, I had the good fortune to receive much valuable advice from Hazard Adams. W. J. T. Mitchell's conversations provided encouragement at a crucial time. I also owe a special debt of gratitude to the work and interest of Jerome McGann.

Colleagues, friends, and family who have given their time unselfishly to help me complete this book include Andrew Barnaby, Alan Bewell, Dave Brady, Janice Carlisle, Alex Gelley, Geoff Harpham, Jim Holstun, Renee Riese Hubert, Diane Lichtenstein, Cynthia Lowenthal, Peter Orelup, Stuart Peterfreund, Mary Poovey, Michael Rothenberg, Norrie Rothenberg, John Carlos Rowe, Ron Schleifer, Maaja Stewart, and Frank Wong. Bob Markley has kept up such enthusiasm and thrown so many good ideas my way over the years that it is impossible to thank him adequately. I would like to return to Martha Cou the boundless affection that her unwavering friendship has given me since I began. Jon Riley has contributed in ways beyond saying, intellectually and emotionally.

Several organizations have given substantial assistance. I wish to thank the National Endowment for the Humanities for the funds to participate in the London seminar; I appreciate the forum for testing my ideas that Lloyd Bitzer and Jim Stoner provided. The Murphy Institute at Tulane University gave me a fellowship to attend John Gray's seminar in liberalism: thanks to Rick Teichgraeber for including me. The editors of *SEL: Studies in English Literature, Genre,* and *Word & Image* graciously permitted me to reprint versions of arguments that first appeared in their journals. The Houghton Library provided the illustrations from *Jerusalem*. I also want to thank the staff at the University of Missouri Press, particularly Tim Fox, for his many insights and improvements, Jane Lago, for her patience and perspicacity, and Beverly Jarrett, who is simply the ideal editor. I am most grateful to Sandy Haro for her cheerful and efficient preparation of the manuscript, and to Paula Rault for her genial cooperation.

This book could not have been completed without Ted Reveley, who has made so much possible for me.

RETHINKING *Blake's* TEXTUALITY

Introduction

In the past decade a gap has opened in Blake studies between commentators who continue to read Blake's poetry as a *work* and those who read it as a *text*, to use Roland Barthes's distinction. Uninterested in seeking the "key" to Blake's system—uninterested in regarding his texts as intentionally unified systems—this latter group (of which the contributors to *Unnam'd Forms: Blake and Textuality, Essential Articles for the Study of William Blake,* and *Blake and the Argument of Method* are exemplary representatives) discloses the fascinatingly anachronistic fact of Blake's "poststructuralism" without indicating what might have enabled it. I argue that Blake arrives at some recognizably poststructuralist positions because he is reponding to the same epistemological crises that continue to shape twentieth-century philosophy. In responding to the issues with which poststructuralism also concerns itself—the subversion of metaphysical presuppositions, the constitution of subjectivity, the ideological mediations that shape forms of consciousness, the nature of semiosis, and the relationship between systematicity and social tyranny—Blake's textual practice implicitly and explicitly participates in a critique of eighteenth-century philosophical assumptions that provides a point of departure for an analysis of the uncomfortable linkages between oppressive actions and "liberatory" resistance.

Blake's work, like some contemporary theory, in effect provides a critique of Kantian deterministic reason and transcendental subjectivity. There is evidence that Blake knew Kant's work: I have found it fruitful to read Blake's own version of deconstructing transcendental subjectivity from within the context of the discursive arena to which Kant also responded. In the process, I have addressed debates over Blake's dualism, his "incoherence," his systematicity, and the status of his "apocalyptic" gestures by reference to other late eighteenth-century documents with which Blake was familiar. By arguing that these documents participate in the elaboration of the epistemological crises of Blake's era, I seek to historicize the links among philosophical discourses of the late eighteenth century, twentieth-century Blake criticism, and current poststructuralist thought. Like the chaos theory of present-day science, Blake's philosophical inquiry into the conditions by which texts/subjects/objects are constituted as meaningful subverts linear and totalizing rationality. I read lines from the conclusion of *Jerusalem*—"the dim Chaos brightend beneath above around! Eyed as the Peacock"—not only as a reference to the Blakean version of a nonlinear, nondeterministic thinking that could displace the absolute position of the subject as it was conceived in traditional Enlightenment terms, but also as Blake's recognition of the dark threat of nondifferentiation lurking in the Enlightenment project of rationalization. Brightening that dim Chaos without producing another form of absolutism or recapitulating the dominating, objectifying *ratio* was the work of Blake's life and remains the avowed task of much contemporary theory.

This book focuses mainly on *Jerusalem*, Blake's last epic poem and the text least treated from a poststructuralist standpoint. In formulating my approach to *Jerusalem*, I have relied on the work of Paul Mann, Nelson Hilton, Donald Ault, Jerome McGann, and Thomas Vogler for theoretical insights and methodological guidance; the particular documents I have juxtaposed to Blake's texts in each of the subsequent sections may be relevant for the other prophetic texts as well. One of the principles guiding my work, however, is that Blake's corpus ought not to be regarded as a unity, as a product of a single intentional activity, nor ought it to be read as furnishing philosophical propositions. The textuality of *Jerusalem* demands that it be performed with careful attention to the rhetorical status of the enunciations from which it is formed and to the intertextual shifts that it both constructs and thematizes. Donald Ault's description of *The Four Zoas*, in some sense the Ur-text of *Jerusalem*, incisively exposes what is at stake in the characterization of these poems' textuality:

> What initially appear to be intra-textual concerns take on the characteristics of a radical intertextualization. The regions of this intertextuality include the revisionary layers and phases of the poem itself. This self-inter-textualization breaks down the metaphor of a

division between an interior and an exterior to the text, because relentlessly close attention to *The Four Zoas* text *enacts* in the reader the same kind of illuminating and exciting cross-referencing that occurs in external contextualization. However it does not *limit* the reader to such possibilities because it does not drive the reader to a fixed external source on which interpretation can rest.[1]

My project differs from Ault's insofar as I do not give an exhaustively minute close reading of the intertextual shifts the textual surface produces. I do, however, follow this method of close reading for the passages I choose as examples of Blake's concerns. The reader need not have read *Jerusalem* in order to follow my argument: one claim my reading of the poem makes is that the poem's strategies and effects can be understood through local specific examples. The reader looking for an "explication" of the poetry will not find one in this study. Instead, I have tried to produce an account of the poem that does not pretend to any kind of "completeness" and that brings to the fore Blake's crucial revisions of and responses to a predominantly philosophical discursive arena that, in his view, constantly contests (or actively represses) the radical implications of the speculations that emerge within it.

At a theoretical level, my argument runs the risk of importing "external sources" as authoritative stabilizers of Blake's "meaning." By indicating some of the intertextual connections that a reader may be led to make by the problems the text poses for a traditional reading practice, I do not mean to suggest that these texts in some sense *are* the ultimate sources of Blake's meaning, nor that they comprise the stages of a history of ideas. In other words, texts such as Alexander Geddes's *Prospectus of a new translation of the Holy Bible*, Thomas Gray's "The Bard," or summaries of Kant's first *Critique* that appeared in Joseph Johnson's *The Analytical Review* are to be understood as participants in the discursive arena with which Blake was familiar, and not as parts of an ahistorically conceived trajectory of intellectual history. The articulations between these texts and Blake's permit me to indicate the radical nature of Blake's thought with respect both to that of his contemporaries and to the philosophical tradition since Kant. I regard Blake's poem in one sense as repre-

---

1. *Narrative Unbound: Re-Visioning William Blake's "The Four Zoas,"* xxiii.

senting a philosophical position enabled by the practices of his era, a position that does not get much elaboration until two-thirds of the way through our century. But in the final analysis, I derive my understanding of that position not from any arguments about Blake's conscious philosophical intentions, but rather from the kinds of concerns I am forced to take up as a consequence of the peculiar textual construction of the poem. Throughout, I have indicated the various options for productive and obstructive reading strategies that my execution of the text has afforded me. Ultimately, then, my argument seeks to make a contribution to contemporary poststructuralist thought as it engages questions of agency and political implication by means of a reading of *Jerusalem*, rather than to proffer an "interpretation" of the poem or an account of what Blake actually intended.

A problem that my description of this text will present for the reader who knows Blake criticism is that it precludes characterizing Blake either as an advocate of traditional liberal political forms or as a prophet of the Utopia of a radical Christian brotherhood. In my view, Blake rejects all attempts to represent any single form as the final stage of history (philosophy, culture, religion); he also rejects the traditional account of the Enlightenment subject as an autonomous, centralized consciousness. I suggest, then, that critics who claim that Blake aims to redeem human society through the transformation of the consciousnesses of individual readers have not taken into account Blake's analysis of the evils produced by utopianism and have misunderstood his evaluations of "possessive selfhood." A great deal of committed humanistic commentary has graced the scholarship devoted to Blake. But on my reading, Blake is a radical critic of the presuppositions of Enlightenment humanism. His criticism stems from an understanding that the Enlightenment humanist or emancipatory project seeks to rationalize and dominate the world as much as any self-legitimated tyranny. The Blake I read cannot transform us into "better" people or lead us through an apocalypse to a new Garden of Eden, but this Blake can provide us with extraordinary means of identifying and exposing the varieties of oppression we foster in the name of Universal Humanity.

So I part company with most Blake scholars, including many poststructuralist critics of Blake, who insist that Blake wishes to give his readers access to a transcendental realm; I also part company with

Introduction 5

my own previously published "self."[2] The refusal of all appeals to authority, the exposure of those appeals as grounded on false or illegitimate premises, and the careful revelation of the strategies by which such appeals are made to appear metaphysically valid—these concerns mark the theoretical project of *Jerusalem*.

This work of Blake's responds to the anxieties about the bases of authority that began to emerge with the English Civil War, as attested to by the welter of radical publication when censorship was lifted in 1642. Suspicions about the right of kings, the authority of the Bible, and the oppressive nature of a constitution that did not recognize the (Christian) egalitarian status of all human beings contributed to the production of new grounds for authority: Baconian science, individual "natural" rights, Quaker Inner Light philosophy, investigations into the role of language in shaping perception, an elevation of the status of historical discourse, and the development of moral philosophy all participated in this production, in the defense against the destabilization of traditional foundations of authority. In each case, Blake has a particular response and a characteristic revision, one that may accept a given analysis but always rejects its inevitable recourse to some ungrounded metaphysics.

Blake's poem begins by problematizing the entire question of authority—divine, authorial, and interpretive; he consistently confronts the reader with his or her own tendency to read by attaching a traditional priority and a standard valence to "transcendent" signifiers such as "Saviour" or "Satan." I have given Part One ("De-Signing Authority") to an exploration of Blake's exposition and subversion of the covert strategies that construct an (illegitimate) metaphysical authority and of the reader's tendency to be complicitous in those constructions. By considering new evidence of Blake's knowledge of the English version of Higher Criticism, I both extend

---

2. Two articles that I published in 1987—"The Provisional Vision of Blake's *Jerusalem*" and "Blake Reads 'The Bard': Contextual Displacement and Conditions of Readability in *Jerusalem*"—are revised and included in this book, but in both cases I arrive at different conclusions than I had previously, particularly with respect to the status of Blake's metaphysical gestures. My recent article "*Jerusalem*'s 'Forgotten Remembrances': A Blakean Analytic of Narrativity and Ideology" represents more accurately the position I take up in this book, one that opposes a multitude of Blake scholars: the only exceptions of whom I am aware are Paul Mann, Donald Ault, Jerome McGann, and Fred Dortort.

and criticize scholarship concerned with defining Blake's use of the Bible.

Part Two ("The Subject of Discourse") takes up the double effects of the destabilization of authority for a Blakean conception of subjectivity and textuality. Here I treat *Jerusalem* within a philosophical context informed by skepticism, associationism, and Kant's transcendentalism, while marking the strategies of exclusion within these philosophical statements as they seek to defend against the radical implications of their analyses by importing transcendentals. This half of the book looks backward to Blake's historical intellectual milieu and forward to the formulations and limitations of phenomenology, deconstructive poststructuralism, and radical feminism as participating in a historically specific discursive arena in which concepts of identity are continually contested, a discursive arena that happens to span two centuries. From this perspective, Blake's textual practice corresponds to an extension of radical skepticism, a path ignored by liberal philosophy after Kant. In the final section of this part ("'The Dim Chaos Brightend' and a Possible Politics of Textuality"), I argue that Blake's analytics of subjectivity and textuality accords with some *post*-poststructuralist insights into the ideological production of a limited, situated, partial subjectivity and the valorization of such a subjectivity as providing the only possible starting place for a nontotalizing and enabling politics. Although this book assumes some familiarity with the classic Blake scholarship, such knowledge is not required to follow the main lines of the argument; the notes give some indication of the ways my argument engages or disrupts the work of other critics. The notes aim as well to provide some supplementary historical information and theoretical speculations. Throughout, my goal has been to derive my arguments from contextualized readings of the poem and then to indicate some of the implications for my understanding of the poem's position for Blake scholarship and for literary theory in order to illuminate the radical importance of *Jerusalem*. Blake struggled to teach us that the world is a perpetually renewed chaos; if this condition occasions our despair, we must learn to see in it our only possibilities for hope.

PART ONE

De-Signing Authority

Inspiration Revised

But in Milton, the Father is Destiny,
the Son, a Ratio of the five senses,
& the Holy-ghost, Vacuum!

Milton, Blake tells us in *The Marriage of Heaven and Hell*, made a mistake when he attributed his inspiration to "the Holy-ghost": "The reason Milton wrote in fetters when he wrote of Angels & God, and at liberty when of Devils & Hell, is because he was a true Poet and of the Devils party without knowing it" (E35).[1] At first it seems that Blake is arguing that the "true Poet" must belong to the Devil's party by default, and his emphasis on the liberating properties of energy and desire—traditionally associated with "deviltry"—in *The Marriage* support that conclusion. But the line also suggests that the distinguishing characteristic of true Poets is their ignorance of the source and authority of their work.[2]

Such a reading might appear perverse, were it not for the stress

---

1. Unless otherwise noted, all references to Blake's texts are taken from *The Complete Poetry and Prose of William Blake*, ed. David V. Erdman, indicated by the abbreviation "E" followed by page numbers. However, I refer to quotations from *Jerusalem* by plate number. My rendering of the punctuation of lines from *Jerusalem* follows that of Copy D, rather than that of *The Complete Poetry and Prose of William Blake*, the punctuation of which was decided upon by reference to several copies. In general, Erdman tends to place commas for periods, colons for semicolons, and exclamation marks for colons. Blake has a clearly delineated comma, with a tail, and a clearly delineated exclamation point, with a tapered line above the final dot. Where the mark on the page is not obviously one or another standard punctuation, I have chosen the punctuation mark that best reproduces in type the mark on the plate of Copy D in order to simulate the difficulties of the reading experience of a particular copy of the poem. The only exception for this is Plate 4's exclamation mark after "brain": although the mark on the page more closely resembles a colon, I believe that the upper end of the exclamation mark was erased with the missing line, which begins "[*Saying*]". Erdman's *The Illuminated Blake* reproduces Copy D.

2. In her "Dancing at the Devil's Party," Alicia Ostriker notes in passing that Blake's idea of a "true Poet" implies that the poet does not know his own mind (3). Although she does not insist on this confusion as defining the true Poet, other scholars (as I discuss below), such as Joseph Wittreich, Leslie Tannenbaum, Geoffrey Hartman, Jerome McGann, and Donald Ault, contribute in various ways to the argument that Blake's radical notion of poetry requires the subversion of the poet's authority.

on this same idea in the address "To the Public" that prefaces *Jerusalem*. There Blake proposes two incompatible sources for the poem. Initially, he places himself in the tradition of epic poets, insofar as the poem was "dictated" to him (E145). He explains, however, that despite the "dictation," he has the option of choosing a variety of cadences, syllables, and styles:

> When this Verse was first dictated to me I consider'd a Monotonous Cadence like that used by Milton & Shak-speare & all writers of English Blank Verse. derived from the modern bondage of Rhyming: to be a necessary and indispensible part of Verse. But I soon found that in the mouth of a true Orator such monotony was not only awkward. but as much a bondage as rhyme itself. I therefore have produced a variety in every line. both of cadences & number of syllables. Every word and every letter is studied and put into its fit place: the terrific numbers are reserved for the terrific parts—the mild & gentle, for the mild & gentle parts. and the prosaic, for inferior parts: all are necessary to each other. (Plate 3)

This passage not only returns to the same metaphorical field linking liberty, creativity, and constraint as the above-cited lines from *The Marriage*, but also undermines our usual sense of the proper relations among those terms. Blake's freedom to create the rhythms and styles of his poem issues precariously from the fact that he did not serve as the poem's origin in the first place *and* from the alleged presence of prearranged positions in the poem where certain styles are necessary and appropriate. In this version of stylistic decorum, Blake's insistence on his freedom is blunted by his apparent agreement with precisely the assumptions about the sources of order in the world and in texts that support the fetters he deplores.

Confusion about the putative origin of the poem emerges again in Plate 4 of chapter one, where one of the narrative voices claims that it sees the "Saviour" daily "Spreading his beams of love, & dictating the words of this mild song." Yet however likely it may seem that the "Saviour" is the source of the poem, the narrator explicitly states that a "theme"—not a being (whether spiritual or mundane)—"calls [him] in sleep night after night" (Plate 4). The situation becomes even more complicated when the conclusion to *Jerusalem* is taken into account, because the last words of the text, "The End of the Song of Jerusalem," indicate that (some of? all of?) what we've been reading originates with Jerusalem herself, even though nothing in the poem has explicitly told us that it has been narrated (or sung, for that matter) by Jerusalem until these final words. Even if we read the "of" as meaning "about," we are still faced with the characterization of the poem as a song, the first mention of which appears in the lines about the Saviour "dictating the words of this mild song." If the Saviour has dictated the words to the "Song of Jerusalem" (which is not, after all, the title of the poem), then the entire poem would be a "mild" song, which contradicts Blake's earlier claim to have created a variety of styles, each in its "fit place." Considering that the speech immediately following the description of the dictating Saviour consists of a series of accusations against Albion, we might well wonder whether the song is mild at all. At the very least, within the first twenty lines of the poem, we do not know who the narrative voice is, whether the narrator claims responsibility for the poem or not, or whether the agency of the poem actually has any authority whatsoever in the characterization or evaluation of the events and personages of the text.

The problem of poetic authority, then, appears both in the address "To the Public" (which we assume to issue from Blake in the character of author of the poem but in which the "author" both claims and disclaims responsibility for the poem) and in the opening lines of the poem proper (which we might reasonably expect to be told from the point of view of a narrative persona but which nonetheless does not clarify the status of that narrator). It is not just a question of "who is speaking?" but also of "who is speaking in the name of what?" Is the poet or narrator inspired—that is, is the poet claiming a special epistemological status? If so, on what grounds? In this poem, the traditionally privileged points of view (transcendent beings, the author speaking for himself) are *at once* foundational and subverted. The undecidable questions of authority that this Blakean strategy institutes have implications not only for any reading of the poem, but for the practice of Blake scholarship as well, since so much of what we think we know of Blake's beliefs derives from our identifying Blake the author with positions adopted by various characters within his poems. In order to begin to determine the function and the effect of this undermining of textual authority, we must look to the historical situation, the philosophical and religious debates concerning authority and inspiration with which Blake was familiar.

Although scriptural authority had been contested increasingly and publicly since the early seventeenth century, the scholarship in biblical criticism in the late eighteenth century to which Blake most often responded focused upon the problem of the authorship of the biblical writings.[3] Historical research and examinations of style made the traditional attribution of authorship of many biblical texts suspect. A number of Higher Critics attempted to preserve the assumption—from a variety of epistemological positions—that access to authorial intent would lead to the discovery of meaning; consequently, they set about the task of ascertaining by historical methods who the real authors of the biblical texts had been. The quest for the meaning of the Bible had to begin with the search for the author. Once the author's identity was validated, then the text could be designated as genuine.

The astonishing result of this effort was that "genuine" no longer meant "expressing God's Word." The role of the individual author took on so much importance that issues of scriptural authenticity were not referred to the question of revelation but simply to historical authorship. The Gospels, then, were to be viewed as authentic not because they contained the Word of God, nor because they were inspired, but because one could determine that they had been written by the apostles.

3. This brief summary of the issues addressed by the Higher Criticism is limited to those critics whose work Blake mentions or who published with Joseph Johnson. I draw my comments from Hans Frei's *The Eclipse of Biblical Narrative: A Study in Eighteenth- and Nineteenth-Century Hermeneutics*, which gives a history of biblical hermeneutics; E. S. Shaffer's *"Kubla Khan" and the Fall of Jerusalem: The Mythological School in Biblical Criticism and Secular Literature, 1770–1880*, which details Coleridge's familiarity with the German Higher Critical principles and suggests Blake's acquaintance with them as well; and Leslie Tannenbaum's *Biblical Tradition in Blake's Early Prophecies: The Great Code of Art*, which verifies Shaffer's speculations vis-à-vis Blake. However, I owe my largest debt for my understanding of the significance of the Higher Criticism in Blake's work to Jerome McGann's "The Meaning of the Ancient Mariner" and "The Idea of an Indeterminate Text: Blake's Bible of Hell and Dr. Alexander Geddes." For an overview of the increasingly destabilized authority of the Scriptures in the seventeenth century, see Christopher Hill's *The World Turned Upside Down: Radical Ideas during the English Revolution*.

Inspiration Revised

Furthermore, critics such as Semler insisted not only that the Bible was not identical with God's Word, but also that the unity of the canon was *historical* rather than divine. As Hans Frei explains, "If the Bible is a library of books from a variety of different contexts, consisting of sometimes conflicting meanings, some more and others less valuable, the choice between them and the criterion for normative religious meaning among all those that emerge out of the variety of these writings is in human rather than divine hands."[4] Interpretation could no longer define itself as the Augustinian task of the recovery of some meaning intended and transmitted by God. The whole issue of authority and authorship in biblical exegesis became secularized, with profound consequences for hermeneutics, as we will see below. This secularization of the Bible by Higher Critical scholarship paved the way for Blake's criticism of "sacred" texts as historical documents of human interpretive choices and rhetorical practices, documents that created an illusion of a unitary canon that would "authorize" oppressive doctrines.

The Higher Criticism eventually broke down the difference between the Bible and secular literature. By determining that the Bible was the work of many authors, these critics created a reading of the Scriptures as part of a body of Oriental literature, rather than as a special genre of revelatory writing, as E. S. Shaffer has shown.[5] This further deprived the Bible of its privileged rank as the literal Word of God. By 1791, Thomas Belsham, the spokesman for the Unitarians and the editor responsible for the policy guiding the publication of the new Unitarian Bible, had accepted the findings of the Higher Criticism that the Pentateuch had a composite authorship and that the creation story was a mythological rendering. The Higher Criticism had found a congenial home among England's Nonconformists.

Johann David Michaelis exposes the interpretive assumptions derived from this scholarship in his appendix to the Unitarian Bible of 1808: "The New Testament is proved to be genuine on the same grounds as the words of profane authors."[6] The Bible's genuineness

---

4. *Eclipse*, 162.
5. "*Kubla Khan*," 26.
6. "Proofs of the Authenticity of the New Testament," 949. Michaelis's *Einleitung in die gottlichen Schriften des neuen Bundes* (1788) is considered to be the seminal expression of the Higher Criticism's methodology and justification, formulating

meant that it was written by authors whose existence could be established on historical or stylistic grounds: the proof of authorship became the hallmark of a work's authenticity. Instead of assuming divine authorship and conferring a privileged status upon the Bible as a consequence, the Higher Critics proposed that the only status the Bible, like any other literary text, could have was as a document whose existence confirmed or made probable the existence of those who authored it in particular historical periods. The truth of the Bible does not inhere in its "revelation" of God's intention, but rather in its having been written by authors whose existence can be proven by historical research, stylistic inquiry, or inference from other texts.

Oddly enough, for the Higher Critics this secularization did not debase the Bible. By examining the Bible as literature, new unities—hitherto unsought and unnoticed—were found to reestablish the preeminence of the biblical word on literary grounds. Bishop Robert Lowth's *Lectures on the Sacred Poetry of the Hebrews* was one of the first works to undertake a comprehensive "critical examination" of the Hebrew poetry from the point of view of metrics, genre, rhetorical figure, and style—in short, from a literary viewpoint.[7] Real men wrote the Scriptures, and because we know who they were, because we know they belonged to a community that chose their writings as reproducing most effectively the experiences described, the integrity and authenticity of the text can be maintained.

As the issue of authority is transformed in the search for authorship, therefore, the question of the truth status of the Bible is displaced. Michaelis goes so far as to release the readers of the Bible from any concern with its revelatory content. He takes a typical

---

the principles of the historical criticism of Johann Gottfried Eichhorn (*Die Urgeschichte*, 1779) and Johann Philipp Gabler. The substance of Michaelis's comments was known in England almost as soon as the German was published. More to the point for the question of Blake's knowledge of the Higher Critical principles, as early as 1771 Joseph Johnson had published an essay of Michaelis's on "the practicability of a universal language"; Johnson also published Herbert Marsh's translation of *Einleitung—Introduction to the New Testament*—from 1793 to 1801.

7. Not all of the historical scholarship of the Bible proposed that it had the same literary status as other myths. Some mythographers, such as Jacob Bryant, argued that the apparent connections between the Bible and other ancient texts were due to the absorption by those other texts of the actual truths presented in the Bible. McGann's brief discussion of this point in "Idea," 312ff., serves as an excellent introduction.

example from the research of the Higher Critics: if we compare Luke's writings to those of Josephus and find chronological errors in the Gospel, "it would militate not against the authenticity of the Acts of the Apostles, but only against the inspiration of the author."[8] In other words, the Gospels are authentic whether or not the apostles were inspired. This is the truly radical gesture of the Higher Criticism: by breaking down the distinction between the secular word of literature and the sacred word of the Scriptures, inspiration is displaced as the origin and unity of the Bible. The conclusions reached by these scholars indicate that inspiration did not produce the Bible, nor is it the mechanism by which truth enters language.

A new use of the term *inspiration* begins to appear as a result of this insistence upon the secular authorship and literary nature of the sacred writings. As Leslie Tannenbaum has demonstrated, Thomas Howes's 1783 commentary on Bishop Lowth's *Lectures* provides an early example of this shift in usage. In considering the mode of Hebraic prophecy—which labels itself "inspired"—Howes considers the question of inspiration to be without interest. He claims that it is more important to determine the historical authenticity of the scriptural writings, as a means of proving their integrity, than it is to wonder whether or not the writers had access to privileged or mystical knowledge of the events. Accordingly, Howes does not even care whether the prophecies were written before or after the event described. His purpose is to free biblical prophetic writing from the charge of irrationality associated with inspiration. But he does so in order to redefine and reinstate "inspiration" as a different type of privileged concept. By showing that the prophecies are rationally *constructed*, he places them in the category of "the best human works," which "approach nearest the divine," and, therefore, can be compared with divine intention. Thus his argument against commentators who see in the prophetic books "a disorder that seemed . . . to render the arrangement unworthy of being ascribed to divine agency" entails a redefinition of inspiration in order to demonstrate the unity of the Bible: the artful construction of the prophecies, not the source of their content, earns them the status of an "inspired" work.[9]

---

8. "Proofs," 950.
9. These quotations from Howes are taken from Tannenbaum, *Biblical Tradition*, 29. See also Tannenbaum's excellent discussion of these issues as they arise

J. G. Eichhorn and J. P. Gabler similarly redefine inspiration and prophecy as products of an artistic construction. Allegory and typology lose their primacy as methods of interpretation because inspiration and divine foreknowledge are no longer at issue. As Shaffer puts it,

> Eichhorn and Gabler banned figura: the Old Testament did not prefigure the New. But they developed a new kind of figura: the New Testament contained the whole of the Old Testament. This was historically rational; yet it preserved the traditional fictional possibilities. Now they take their start in Revelation after the fact, in short, in apocalypse, not in "prophecy." Prophecy is no longer the prediction of actual events to come, but the renewed vision of the meaning of the past for the future.[10]

That is, the Higher Critics offer a way of rereading the Bible that emphasizes the New Testament's *revision* of the Old Testament. Instead of the traditional exegetical view that the Old Testament predicts or contains all of the New Testament, the Higher Critical view proposes that we regard the writing of the New Testament as a deliberate incorporation of the Old. For those who believe in it, the New Testament gives the Old Testament a new context, which *constructs* the appearance of a unified text.

In this version of the Scriptures as revision, prophecy is not the product of inspiration but rather an interpretation that produces what we might call the "effect of inspiration." By creating the semblance of a unified text out of discrete parts, each of which claims sacred status and each of which presents its own interpretation of prior "sacred" texts, a post hoc unity is imposed upon the event or text being interpreted or "prophesied" that stands as the sign of its allegedly divine source. In a vast departure from traditional versions of inspiration, where the secular author contributes nothing

---

in Lowth and Howes in his chapter entitled "Prophetic Form," especially 28–33. Although he is not concerned centrally with the problem of defining inspiration, Tannenbaum does show that the concept of coherence is linked closely to that of intentionality and therefore that any charges of "incoherence" against a text reputed to be the product of divine inspiration would have to be countered by redefining "coherence" or "inspiration" or both.

10. *"Kubla Khan,"* 138.

but his body as a channel for divine communication, this definition says that textual markers that indicate the intervention of the author signify "inspiration." Because the author is writing an interpretation of previous texts, and working to produce the impression that the older text and his text emanate from the same external, all-knowing source, "inspiration" comes to refer not to the genesis of the text but rather to an interpretive effect—it is a function of the text's rhetorical power rather than a function of the ontology of the text.

One consequence of this shift in the definition of interpretation, as I will discuss below in relation to Blake's work, is that it transforms concerns about recovering "intended meaning" into concerns about rhetorical ends. I call this the displacement of hermeneutics by rhetoric. Referring to the work of Eichhorn and Schleiermacher, for example, Shaffer notes that "apostolic authorship depended on canonicity, and canonicity ultimately on inspiration *in the new sense of the capacity to recreate the experience of faith.*"[11] What is at stake is whether "inspiration" means that the text presents God's truth as an a priori guarantee of meaning, or whether inspiration gets attributed to the text, regardless of the poet's assertions, by virtue of some interpretive effect and/or rhetorical strategy. The criterion that inspiration "recreate imaginatively the experience of faith" cannot be assumed before reading the text. It derives from the persuasive power of the text itself, not from some quality of "truth" instilled in the text by its author.[12] In her study of Coleridge's relationship to the Higher Critics, Shaffer concludes that it is "neither the unquestioned authority of the Church nor the unquestioned authority of the biblical text on which tradition rests, but the perpetually shifting sense within the Christian community *of what has the power to persuade its members* and strengthen them in the faith."[13] The abiding interest of the Bible, then, emerges from its *rhetorical*—not its hermeneutical—message. The Bible is a compendium of rhetorical strategies for producing the impression of a "divine" status, not

---

11. Ibid., 85, my emphasis.
12. Schleiermacher wrote a generation after Michaelis, but his *Hermeneutik* depends for its interpretive principles upon the historical criticism of the previous age (cf. Frei, *Eclipse*, 284ff.). In Schleiermacher's work we see the issue of persuasion that is implicit in his predecessors brought to the fore, as it is in both Coleridge and Blake (see also McGann, "Ancient Mariner").
13. "Kubla Khan," 85–86, my emphasis.

communications from the empyrean about future events or eternal truths.

My understanding of this shift from the hermeneutical to the rhetorical is shaped by Jerome McGann's analysis of Coleridge's adoption of Higher Critical principles. For Coleridge, according to McGann, the Scriptures "do not represent a 'true' narrative of certain fixed original events; rather, they are a collection of poetic materials which represent the changing form of 'witness' or testament of faith created by a religious community in the course of its history."[14] I read "changing form of 'witness'" to mean changing rhetorical strategies and criteria for credibility, for *persuasion*. For Coleridge, the Bible is a historical record of these changes; for Blake, as we will see, the Bible is a historical record of the means by which "sacred" texts are constructed to oppress. Like the Higher Critics and Coleridge, Blake believed that the Scriptures were records of rhetorical strategies for creating a unified community, for establishing authority, and for producing an ideologically coherent text. Unlike the Higher Critics and Coleridge, Blake indicates that this ideological coherence was not only simulated but designed to repress. Where the Higher Critics saw a progression from one to another "form of witness," Blake saw a continued tendency for mankind to mislead and oppress itself, to create gods and forget their secular origin: "Thus men forgot that All deities reside in the human breast" (*The Marriage*, E38).

Blake's Higher Criticism and the Art of Inspiration

When the term *inspiration* occurs in Blake's work, it has a double significance, for it is both rhetorically strategic, proposing a special status for the work, and a relocation or redefinition of the issue of poetic authority. Blake's strategic use of "inspiration"

---

14. "Ancient Mariner," 48.

emerges most clearly in his examination of the assumptions of the Higher Criticism, which he discovered through his friendship with Joseph Johnson, the publisher of many of the proponents of the Higher Criticism, most notably Michaelis, Joseph Priestley, and Geddes.[15]

In his annotations to Bishop Watson's *An Apology for The Bible . . . addressed to Thomas Paine*, Blake reveals his knowledge of the Higher Criticism and its implications.[16] Throughout his commentary, Blake demonstrates his understanding that "authority" (the power of the text to move its audience) can be distinct from "authenticity" (the question of the origin of the text). By displacing the question of authority from issues concerning a text's origin in some transcendental sphere to its rhetorical effects, the Higher Criticism provides Blake with the connection between inspiration and artful construction (or "fabrication" or "design," to use the terms that emerge from the annotations to Watson) that marks the opening to *Jerusalem*.

Watson's *Apology* attacks *The Age of Reason*, where Paine argues that the Bible recorded only ancient fictions, not historical truth. Watson, in his argument against Paine, also argues against the Higher Criticism by distinguishing between "genuineness," or the correct attribution of an author to his writing, and "authenticity," or the truth of the writing regardless of authorial attribution. Watson thinks that this distinction will salvage the truth value of the Bible in the face of scholarship showing that certain sections of it could not have been written by their accepted authors. Part of Paine's argument concerning the fabricated nature of the Bible rests on the Higher Critical finding that the books of Moses, Joshua, and Samuel had composite authorship, so Watson's definition of authenticity seeks

15. In addition to the many works of Priestley and the important *Introduction to the New Testament* of Michaelis that were published by Johnson, Geddes's *Proposals for printing by a subscription a new translation of the Holy Bible, from corrected texts of the originals* (1788) contained an extensive scholarly exposition of the Higher Criticism's historical research into the authorship, redaction, and translation of the Scriptures in their various versions. Johnson also published Geddes's translation of the Bible in 1790, his *General answer* to his critics upon his publication of his prospectus for his new translation in 1790, his *Address to the Public* on the publication of the first volume of his new translation of the Bible in 1793, and his *Critical remarks on the Hebrew Scriptures* in 1800.

16. See Tannenbaum, *Biblical Tradition*, 28, for a different look at the annotations to Watson's letters as evidence for Blake's knowledge of the Higher Criticism.

to counter Paine's claim that composite authorship subverts the authority of these Scriptures.

According to Blake, Watson's response to Paine's charges makes trivial distinctions. Blake agrees with Paine that the discovery of misattribution undermines the authority of the works in question: "He who writes things for true which none would write. but the actor. such are most of the acts of Moses. must either be the actor or a fable writer or a liar. *If Moses did not write the history of his acts. it takes away the authority altogether* it ceases to be history & becomes a Poem . . ." ("Annotations to *An Apology for the Bible*," E616, my emphasis). Blake here recognizes the strength of the argument against authority: if the Bible is literary, if it is constructed, its only authority derives from its rhetorical force. The power of the Scriptures, then, would not be a concomitant of divine power but a function of the rhetorical skills of its author and of the use to which it is put. Blake criticizes Watson's failure to see the cogency of Paine's arguments that

> the books of the Bible were never believd willingly by any nation & that none but designing Villains ever pretended to believe That the Bible is all a State Trick, thro which tho' the People at all times could see they never had. the power to throw off Another Argument is that all the Commentators on the Bible are Dishonest Designing Knaves who in hopes of a good living adopt the State religion this he has shewn with great force . . . ("Annotations," E616)

The corollary term for fabrication—the mark of the loss of divine authority—is *design*. Because the Bible is the artful construction of men posing as divine vehicles, it loses its unity as the Word of God (that unity is simply a product of the compositional strategies), becoming instead a fabricated unity, designed as a "State Trick" in the service of obtaining power.[17]

17. Donald Ault has pointed out to me that the syntax of this passage suggests an alternative reading, viz. that only designing villains pretend to believe that the Bible is all a state trick. Blake's ability to put his readers into uncomfortable situations cannot be denied; this alternative reading characterizes any reader adopting the interpretation I am advancing as a "designing villain." I would argue that Blake's interest in Paine's argument focuses less on Paine's ethical judgment of villainy and more on his description of the processes by which language comes to appear as the transparent medium of truth. Paine seems to

This is the context in which Blake reintroduces the term *inspiration*. In the annotation directly succeeding Blake's comments on the secular construction of the Bible, Blake links "fabrication" and "inspiration" with loss of authority: "If Moses did not write the history of his acts. it takes away the authority altogether it ceases to be history & becomes a Poem of probable impossibilities fabricated for pleasure as moderns say but I say by Inspiration" ("Annotations," E616). "Inspiration" comes to stand for the ability of the writer to produce the effect of authenticity by adopting the position (name, stance, strategy) of what traditional biblical hermeneutics calls the "author." The "authority" that is lost is the authority Bishop Watson desperately asserts: some bedrock guarantee that the text presents the truth despite the text's apparent implausibility. In this passage, Blake seems to agree that textual authority derives from authentic authorship, but the Aristotelian echo implies—and other passages confirm—that Blake is developing a theory of the relationship between language and power that bypasses questions of authenticity, originary intention, or truth altogether. Blake wants to maintain the force of the term *inspiration* as an index of the power of the text without committing himself to a model of textual authority that ultimately involves an appeal to metaphysical transcendentals.

Throughout the annotations to Watson's *Apology*, Blake alludes to ethos and pathos as the source of a text's authority; rhetorical force counts as inspiration, whether the text is put to use for pleasure or villainy:

> Is it a greater miracle to feed five thousand men with five loaves than to overthrow all the armies of Europe with a small pamphlet. (E617)
>
> Every honest man is a Prophet he utters his opinion both of private & public matters (E617)
>
> [Paine] says that Moses being proved not the author of that history which is written in his name & in which he says I did so & so Undermines the veracity intirely the writer says he is Moses if this is proved false the history is false Deut xxxi v 24 But perhaps Moses is not the author & then the Bishop loses his Author (E616)

---

believe that there is an alternative to the ideological use of language; Blake, as I show below, has no such illusions.

> I cannot concieve the Divinity of the <books in the> Bible to consist either in who they were written by or at what time or in the historical evidence which may be all false in the eyes of one man & true in the eyes of another but in the Sentiments & Examples which whether true or Parabolic are Equally useful as Examples given to us . . . (E618)

In these passages, it appears that writing in the name of God is the same as writing in the name of Moses; both are equally inspired, that is to say, both are determined by the goal of persuading readers. Neither, if we follow the implications of Blake's commentary, derives its power from any divine origin but only from knowledge of rhetorical techniques for producing the illusion of an original, authoritative voice. The annotations indicate that Blake's knowledge of Higher Critical principles (concerning the composite nature of the Bible and the questions of authenticity and authority that follow from it) helps ground his interest in the rhetorical power effected by invoking traditional concepts of authority and inspiration and by the application of persuasive strategies that will produce the conditions of belief in the reader.

Not only the Bible itself, but commentary on the Bible as well—the entire tradition of exegesis—partakes of the same designing ends and uses the same rhetorical strategies. By the time Blake writes the address "To the Public" in *Jerusalem*, the marks of Blake's intervention in what traditionally was believed to be the transmission of divine words through the poet serve to distinguish the poem *as* "inspired"; at the same time, Blake situates himself within a tradition that considered "inspired prophecy" and "inspired exegesis" to consist in a certain style of composition. Leslie Tannenbaum's discussion of Thomas Howes's analysis of the disunity of the biblical prophecies helps illuminate Blake's use of this technique as a sign of inspiration.[18]

---

18. All quotations from Howes can be found in Tannenbaum, *Biblical Tradition*, especially 28–36. Tannenbaum gives a reading of the address "To the Public" by reference to Howes in order to establish Blake's awareness of prophecy as a particular rhetorical style, as *oratory*. Tannenbaum suggests that Blake uses the ordering principles that Howes and others find in the biblical prophecies to create the coherence of his own work. My objection to this reading is that it establishes the coherence of Blake's text on the basis of mimesis rather than rhetoric. In other words, while Tannenbaum argues that Blake's apparent incoherence is designed to draw attention to its resemblance to the incoherence of

Howes addresses the question of the unity of the prophecies as a function of style. He does not deny that the biblical prophecies appear disordered if considered in the chronological order of presentation. But, he says, previous commentators (from Lowth to Le Clerc) failed to consider two other ways to make sense of the "irregular jumble" of the prophetic writings: ". . . for there are at least two other kinds of order, and both preferable, viz. that of *historic order* in which the prophecies were accomplished, also that *oratorical order* which might be thought best suited to the purpose of *persuasion and argumentation*." Later, Howes equates the oratorical order with poetic arrangement, showing that "there are equally good reasons to conceive these prophecies to be put together in a connected method and order, agreeably to such modes of poetic and oratorical arrangement." Tannenbaum explains that the difficulty of the historical order is that "whenever the prophet claims that a prophecy has been fulfilled by a specific event, he becomes a fallible interpreter of previous prophecies rather than the communicator of inspired truths," an objection that Howes himself raises. The purpose of the oratorical order, then, is to "establish the credibility" of the prophet; Tannenbaum further suggests that Howes's preference for the oratorical order is to shift the issue of prophecy from its predictive to its persuasive function, to establish credibility by rhetorical means. In so doing, the entire definition of inspired prophecy moves away from the revelation of divine truths and future events to the construction of a certain type of text that cites and interprets previous "authoritative" texts in a bid to transfer their authority to itself: "This oratorical order could also include the citation of the fulfillment of a previous prophecy by an earlier prophet or by the prophet himself in order to establish the veracity of a new prophecy that he was about to make." Thus, the "inspired" prophecy is produced by an "orator" who knows how to insert himself in the tradition of exegesis for the (same) purpose of obtaining the confidence of his audience.[19]

In the annotations to Watson's *Apology*, Blake discusses the con-

---

Biblical prophecies, I argue that Blake's reference to oratory in the address, and his careful staging of an impossibly coherent incoherence, serves to call attention to the rhetorical level of the work—its artful composition, its production of a "reader" function, and its interest in the construction of authority.

19. *Biblical Tradition*, 31 and 32.

nection between prophecy and rhetoric: "Prophets in the modern sense of the word have never existed Jonah was no prophet in the modern sense for his prophecy of Nineveh failed" ("Annotations," E617). For Blake, prophecy is not the unmediated transmission of a "Divine Voice," but rather the art of establishing the prophet as a credible communicator, one who will be believed. He arranges or constructs his work in order to create the conditions in which belief will be fostered. He has "designs" upon his audience, just as Paine contended, although he may work his wiles for beneficent ends. In short, there is nothing of the "miraculous" in the prophecies.

Such were Christ's miracles, which Blake equates with the miracles of persuasion wrought by Paine's *Age of Reason:*

> Jesus could not do miracles where unbelief hindered hence we must conclude that the man who holds miracles to be ceased puts it out of his own power to ever witness one The manner of a miracle being performd is in modern times considerd as an arbitrary command of the agent upon the patient but this is an impossibility not a miracle neither did Jesus ever do such a miracle. Is it a greater miracle to feed five thousand men with five loaves than to overthrow all the armies of Europe with a small pamphlet. look over the events of your own life & if you do not find that you have both done such miracles & lived by such you do not see as I do True I cannot do a miracle thro experiment & to domineer over & prove to others my superior power as neither could Christ . . . how can Watson ever believe the above sense of a miracle who considers it as an arbitrary act of the agent upon an unbelieving patient. whereas the Gospel says that Christ could not do a miracle because of Unbelief ("Annotations," E616–17)

Blake follows the Higher Critical shift from transcendent to secular (Christ and Blake are the same in their inability to perform miracles) and from truth to persuasion. The key to all prophecy that claims an "inspired" status is that it works by producing the conditions for belief. The events of the prophecies have no ontological priority or authority; they have only rhetorical force.

Blake's statement in the *Laocoon* that "The Old & New Testaments are the Great Code of Art" suggests that his interest in the Bible derives from the history of its interpretation, a history that is already inscribed in the Bible (E274). Read in light of the Higher Criticism's analysis that "the New Testament contained the whole of the Old Testament," Blake's use of "Code" alludes to its meaning, derived from "codex," as any one of several ancient manuscript volumes of the Scriptures.[20] The variants in the codices form the basis for the Higher Criticism's discussion of the Scriptures as collections of writings, revisions, and commentary. The Bible, then, is not just a volume containing a compendium of patterns, forms, and images that the artist may decipher, but rather an artful construction, composed from the processes of translation, redaction, and interpretation, contriving to make multiplicity (several variants, two Testaments) function as a unity. Art, in Blake's aphorism, defines itself as the fabrication of unity—and consequently of authority—by revision, recontextualization, and interpretation. This mode of revision appears everywhere in Blake's work. His marginalia are emendations, correctives, con-texts. When Blake claims to read the Bible in its "diabolical" sense, when he tells the Deists in "The Everlasting Gospel" that he reads white where they read black, we cannot be content with critical views that describe Blake's use of the Bible in mimetic terms. For Blake, the Bible and its exegesis exemplify a strategy for producing authority—for producing sacred texts. This is the "prophetic" mode as Blake conceived it, analogous to the oratorical order described by Howes.

What makes the "sacred" texts so powerful is not simply their revisionary stance, but their internal representation of a history of interpretation. In order to persuade its readers to a new understanding of the importance and authority of older texts, every prophecy interprets and revises its predecessor texts, usually to produce a new context that highlights the tradition of continuing authority as it "emerges" in the newly constructed prophecy. Newton presents the classical explanation of the peculiar format of the prophecies: "all of them together make but one complete Prophesy [that] consists of two parts, an introductory Prophesy, and an Interpretation thereof."[21] Commenting on the relevance of this passage for Blake, Joseph Wittreich notes that Newton's description was acceptable to Blake because "each prophet is both creator of his visions and inter-

20. Shaffer, *"Kubla Khan"*, 138.
21. The quotation from Newton's *Observations* can be found in Joseph Anthony Wittreich, Jr., "Opening the Seals," 30.

preter of them; and every subsequent prophet repeats the pattern but, in the process, becomes an interpreter both of his own visions and of the visions of his predecessors." Hence, in this description there is no distinction between prophecy and interpretation. The Bible functions not only as a repository of forms, images, plots, and patterns—the terms in which most commentators have viewed the Bible's significance for Blake—but also as a collection of interpretations and revisions that signal the construction of authority by the writer who wishes to produce the effect of "sacredness."

Wittreich makes a case for Blake's knowledge of the interpretive structure of prophecy, suggesting that Blake could have been familiar with Pareus's commentary on the prophecies through Milton's writings. According to Pareus, the prophet gives the reader two locations for the meaning of the prophecy: first, in the prologue or explanation of the vision, and second, in the vision itself, presented to "exercise the mind to truth." In this formulation, we find echoes of Blake's belief that obscure material "rouzes the faculties to act." Pareus's commentary, as presented by Wittreich, implies that the prophet is a creator of the vision, but at the same time the vision brings the viewer and the reader to a transcendent truth. In this reading, the traditional meaning of the term *inspiration* is at work. Although this discussion is useful for understanding how Blake's text employs versions of the same event for the purposes of instructing his readers in the "fabricated" nature of prophetic writing, Wittreich throughout continues to employ the traditional usage of inspiration as the equivalent of divine communication, a status he accords to Blake's texts as well as to the biblical prophecies. This is a Romantic position in that it postulates a realm of transcendence. For Wittreich, the important point is that Pareus outlines the structural elements of Revelation that serve as a model for *Jerusalem*. On his view, the apparent disunity of Blake's poem derives from its model and hence is not disunity or incoherence at all. By positing that Blake's texts bear a mimetic relationship to the Bible (as does Tannenbaum), Wittreich misses the moments in Pareus (and in Blake) that undermine the notion of inspiration as communication with an external, independent authority.

According to Pareus, the would-be prophet has to produce his own authority to insure his credibility: "It is one thing to write prophesie . . . the truth of an historie requireth not the authority of the writer . . . a prophesie does." The creation of authority is the prerequisite for the audience's participation in the interpretive process, necessary before they can "engage in the mental warfare that produces apocalypse."[22] As part of their strategy for gaining authority, then, prophecies represent their own interpretive acts, instructing their readers in the hermeneutic procedures necessary to constitute readings that have the "mark of authority." In order to persuade their readers that they have the authority to revise other prophecies, the writers of the prophecies demonstrate the revisionary and rhetorical nature of all prophecy. Thus, the basis for hermeneutical activity, as represented in the Scriptures, is a rhetorically constructed authority. Without rhetorical analysis, no credibility; without credibility, no interpretive "truth." Rhetoric—not divine agency—is the source of biblical authority.

Sheep and Goats: Disseminating Authority

*I*f prophecies establish their authority on the basis that authority itself is rhetorically constituted in "sacred" texts, then authority can be disseminated through texts, independent of divine agency. Every prophet becomes "inspired" by the rhetoric of authority in his predecessor texts, while those texts themselves demonstrate the means for disseminating authority. The Scriptures offer numerous examples of this mechanism of dissemination, which serves to guarantee the reproduction and the distribution of the predecessor text by means of textual instruction. For example, in Deuteronomy 11:18, the Pentateuch attempts to ensure its own perpetuation as follows:

> Therefore shall ye lay up these my words in your heart and in your soul, and bind them for a sign upon your hand, that they

---

22. Both quotations from Pareus are in Wittreich, "Opening the Seals," 35.

> may be as frontlets between your eyes. And ye shall teach them to your children, speaking of them when thou walkest by the way, when thou liest down, and when thou risest up. And thou shalt write them upon the door posts of thine house and upon thy gates. . . . Behold, I set before you this day a blessing and a curse. A blessing if ye obey the commandments of the Lord your God, which I command you this day: And a curse if ye will not obey the commandments of the LORD your God. . . . [23]

The text cites as part of the Lord's commandments the provision that those commandments be eternally reproduced. Any text that can attach itself to the Old Testament as part of the Word of God could automatically be reproduced by this provision. In Revelation 22:19, the same injunctions are expressed: "And if any man shall take away from the words of the Book of this prophecy, God shall take away his part out of the book of life, and out of the holy city, and from the things which are written in this book." Here the domain is entirely textual. The text of the Book of Revelation guarantees one's reproduction in the book of life, an event which derives its importance from the *original* book, the "sacred" book.

These instructions demonstrate an attempt to consolidate and maintain an "authoritative" text, but they also exemplify places where the Scriptures reveal their rhetorical construction as a series of interpretations, each of which authorizes itself by reference to the dissemination of authority written into its predecessor. The first book of the New Testament provides the paradigmatic manifestation of the necessity for constructing an authority derived from—and superior to—the Old Testament. Direct references to passages in Matthew outnumber all references to the other apostles in Blake's corpus; significantly, *Jerusalem* itself opens with an obvious allusion to Matthew in the form of the words SHEEP and GOATS flanking the title "To the Public." Because many of the chapters in Matthew are concerned with the problem of the origin of Jesus' authority, this Gospel is well suited to helping Blake articulate his ambiguous attributions of authorship at the opening of the poem.

If we go directly to Matthew 21:23–27, which treats Jesus' authority explicitly, we find at issue precisely the question of whether Jesus'

---

23. All citations from the Bible are taken from the King James version unless otherwise noted.

authority derives from God or whether he is simply arrogating to himself an illicit authority. When the Pharisees pose the question, "By what authority doest thou these things? and who gave thee this authority?" Jesus understands that they are implying that any authority not obtained directly from a divine source amounts to nothing more than the illegitimate assumption of authority. In order to demonstrate the Pharisees' misconception about the nature of authority, Jesus proposes a test for *them* by which he will determine whether or not to reveal the source of his own authority: "I also will ask you one thing, which if ye tell me, I in like wise will tell you by what authority I do these things. The baptism of John, whence was it? from heaven, or of men?" The test, appropriately enough, concerns the determination of the source of authority for a prophet. Here Jesus apparently concurs with the Pharisaic assumption that only God can confer legitimate authority. In response, the Pharisees reason that if they say John's authority was from heaven, Jesus will inquire why they did not believe John's teaching, while, on the other hand, if they say that John's authority was nothing more than human presumption, the mob, who believe in John's prophecies, will attack the Pharisees: "And they reasoned with themselves, saying, If we shall say, From heaven: he will say unto us, Why did ye not then believe him? But if we shall say, Of men; we fear the people; for all hold John as a prophet." The second answer implies that John was a kind of charlatan who has fooled the masses, which is evidently the Pharisees' opinion. Caught between their fear of revealing their hypocrisy and their fear of the people, they respond, "We cannot tell," to which Jesus replies, "Neither tell I you by what authority I do these things."

Jesus knows the source of his authority, but the Pharisees do not know the source of John's. Nonetheless, Jesus' statement produces an equivalence between John's authority and his own. His words ought to indicate to the Pharisees that Jesus' authority is like John's, neither guaranteed by heavenly authority nor self-assumed. John's authority, like Jesus', proceeds from men who believe in his authority. In fact, the Pharisees' unwillingness to answer Jesus for fear of reprisals from the people *confirms* this alternative, since it is the people's belief in John's authority that endangers the Pharisees. Jesus has only asked the Pharisees to reply, not to reply with the correct answer: the Pharisees are trapped by the false dilemma they themselves have produced. Their insistence upon divine authority as the guarantee of absolute answers and eternal interpretations comprises the chains that bind their minds, forcing them into silence. As Jesus remarks time and again in this Gospel, the conditions for his works is faith: the belief in his authority—not the origin of it—creates his authority. As an indicator of Blake's sense of the importance of conditions of belief for the production of authority, we can refer back to Blake's assertion that Christ's miracles depended upon the rhetorical skill of the prophet in persuading his audience to believe in him.

Rather than insisting upon an absolute authority who can guarantee meanings and interpretations, the Jesus of Matthew appropriates that authority, and then—the crucial gesture for my reading of the opening of *Jerusalem*—disseminates that authority among his listeners. This is the strategy of the parable of the sheep and the goats, recounted in Matthew 25:31–46, a rhetorical strategy that proposes—and then subverts—a set of authoritative positions from which interpretations gain their validity. This strategy, I argue, serves Blake throughout *Jerusalem*.

In the opening plate of the poem, Blake places his readers in a familiar interpretive situation when he inscribes SHEEP and GOATS at the top of the address "To the Public," for the public will know that parables always call for interpretation and that Jesus is traditionally presented as the interpretive authority within the parables. In this instance, the reader seems to be asked to identify with the sheep, the "righteous" in the parable, as part of the parable's promise of eternal salvation:

> When the Son of man shall come in his glory, and all the holy angels with him, then shall he sit upon the throne of his glory:
> And before him shall be gathered all nations: and he shall separate them one from another, as a shepherd divideth his sheep from his goats:
> And he shall set the sheep on his right hand, but goats on the left.
> Then shall the King say unto them on his right hand, Come ye blessed of my Father, inherit the kingdom prepared for you from the foundation of the world:

However, in Matthew as well as in *Jerusalem*, the identification of the righteous is complicated by at least three problems.

First, the parable makes clear that those who are sheep and those who are goats *do not know who they are*. After explaining that the righteous deserve salvation for their charitable actions toward the Son of man, the Jesus of Matthew prophesies:

> Then shall the righteous answer him, saying, Lord, when saw we thee an hungered, and fed thee? or thirsty, and gave thee drink?
> When saw we thee a stranger, and took thee in? or naked, and clothed thee?
> Or when saw we thee sick, or in prison, and came unto thee?

Only the Son of man may point out who belongs in which category. In fact, as Matthew 25:31 asserts, the distinguishing characteristic of the sheep is that they cannot know they are righteous until "the Son of man shall come in all his glory." That time cannot be the time of the speaking of the parable (nor can it be Blake's time), for the Son had not yet come in all his glory with all the angels. The parable tells its readers that people are ignorant of their own moral status and will remain so until the Son of man returns to interpret them to themselves. So the point at which the parable holds out knowledge to its readers is also the point at which it reiterates their ignorance.

Second, even though the parable seems to propose a method for achieving the reward of eternal life—by being righteous—this method involves an action on the part of the audience that inevitably contradicts the explicit message of the parable. In order to belong to the category of the righteous, the auditor is supposed to treat all men as part of Christ, as belonging to one category. In response to the questions of the righteous, the Son of man replies, "Verily I say unto you, Inasmuch as ye have done it unto one of the least of these my brethren, ye have done it to me." The determining criterion for righteousness, apart from one's lack of knowledge about being righteous, is acting upon the identification of all men in Christ. However, those who treat all men as Christ so that they can be counted as sheep and not as goats have already violated the moral of the parable, for they have posited, and acted on, a division in humanity.

Third, and most problematic, the attempt to avoid becoming a goat appropriates the Son of man's position as the interpreter. On the one hand, the parable authorizes this appropriation of the role of the interpreter, since all men are identified in Christ; on the other hand, the parable forbids the gesture, since the separation of sheep and goats depends upon a transcendent viewpoint that will come at a later time. Unless the Son of man is granted a special status (i.e., unlike all other men, a status which would make it impossible for men to "identify" with Christ), then the injunction of the parable to treat all men as Christ has no force, because it devolves from no authority such as that promised in the deferred fulfillment of the parable. Yet if the Son of man is granted this special status, the "identification" cannot take place.

The reader of the parable (or of the opening of *Jerusalem*) has the option of trying to enter the Kingdom of Heaven by ignoring these problems and identifying himself or herself as a "sheep." The interpretation of the parable that calls for the sheep to separate themselves in the here and now from the goats relies on an authoritative Son of man at the end of days to make everything come out all right. In effect, this projected position of an ideal authoritative interpreter simply provides the alibi for the seizure of interpretive authority by those who wish to be sheep, at the moment that they are caught in the double bind of the parable. Blake's solution to this paradox is to offer his readers the opportunity to revise their understanding of the apparently transcendental interpretive authority that the parable posits as both necessary and impossible, as salvation and damnation.

Blake begins by reminding his readers that they must become interpreters themselves, not only by presenting them with the allusion to the parable but also by making it possible to read the inscription as suggesting that "the Public" consists of both sheep and goats.[24] Then, in the body of the address Blake explicitly rejects the moral project of the traditional reading of the parable: "and he who waits to be righteous before he enters into the Saviours kingdom. the Divine Body: will never enter there." He even goes so far as to identify himself as one of the wicked: "I am perhaps the most sinful

---

24. In fact, in the manuscript of notebooks written between 1808 and 1811, Blake criticizes the Jesus of Matthew on precisely this point: "Jesus . . . makes a Wide Distinction between the Sheep & the Goats consequently he is Not Charitable" (E695). However, it is always risky to take Blake's statements out of their immediate context, as I argue in subsequent sections.

of men! I pretend not to holiness! yet I pretend to love. to see. to converse with daily. as man with man. & the more to have an interest in the Friend of Sinners." (Plate 3). Blake rejects the criterion of righteousness as a mark distinguishing those who are part of Christ and those who are not. In the process, he rejects the notion that there are two categories of men—those who will enter the Kingdom of Heaven and those who will not: "The Spirit of Jesus is continual forgiveness of Sin:" (Plate 3).

Further, Blake short-circuits the delay implicit in the parable, for, according to him, no one will have to wait to enter into the Divine Body. That is, Blake takes away the narrative dimension of the parable by removing both the absence of the Son of man—the lack which the narrative of the parable proposes in order to claim a future amelioration—and the distinction between the sheep and the goats that generates the play of interpretation—the gap instituted by the narrative to maintain narrativity itself. Thus, the audience that was both divided and unitary with respect to the interpretive authority of the parable becomes unified in a decisive interpretive gesture on Blake's part, with the consequence that the position of transcendental authority cannot be maintained. Everyone is a part of Christ, and there is no Christ without this global identification. For Blake, granting a transcendental authority above man is a sin above all others, since that position always authorizes an uncharitable distinction between human beings, a distinction not permitted by an identification in Christ. By taking on the role of interpreter, Blake also implicitly criticizes the parable's apparent command to divide present and future, sheep and goats, nations and Son of man, the living world and the Kingdom of Heaven: entrance to the Divine Body cannot be contingent.

By displacing a transcendent viewpoint as the interpretive authority in his text, Blake produces an interesting revision of the traditional reading of the parable of the sheep and goats. Where the Son of man is reified and given a special transcendent status in the parable, humanity is divided. Where the Son of man is understood to refer to all humanity identified in Christ, that centralized authority is destroyed and a reciprocal relationship is established among men. In the address "To the Public," Blake calls that reciprocity "the Spirit of Jesus." Blake's authority, then, is derived: he is "inspired" by the Spirit of Jesus, and therefore "authorized" to correct or revise the parable.

It is worth noting that the Gospel has already pointed the way to this strategy. During Jesus' temptation in the wilderness, the devil asks Jesus to assert his authority as the Son of God by imposing on the order of nature. Jesus replies, "Scripture says, man does not live by bread alone." Here Jesus does not speak for himself, but through scriptural quotation, and in so doing identifies himself not as the Son of God, but as a man. Jesus does not triumph over the devil by asserting his unique identity and special status, but by identifying with mankind through a recontextualization of the words of a precedent authoritative text.

Blake undoes the interpretive knot of the parable of the sheep and the goats by displacing its ostensible hermeneutic authority. A single source guaranteeing a unified interpretation, true for all time, gives way to readers who, following the parable, displace its authority onto themselves. The dissemination of transcendent authority to the secular, multiple audience, however, creates a crisis. Frank Kermode, in addressing this situation in scriptural studies, proposes that any position that acknowledges the inaccessibility of one "intended" meaning implicitly authorizes a variety of individual interpretations. Kermode calls this position an "outsider's theory"—thereby signaling his belief in the distinction between insiders (who have access to an intended meaning) and outsiders (who don't). Kermode's description, if not his complaint, serves to elucidate my point:

> It stems ultimately from a Protestant tradition, that of the devout dissenter animated only by the action of the spirit, abhorring the claim of the institution to an historically validated traditional interpretation. It may be the end of that tradition; for I do not see how, finally, it can distinguish between sacred and secular texts, those works of the worldly canon that also appear to possess inexhaustible hermeneutic potential.[25]

The hermeneutic that posits an infinitude of "correct" interpretations—interpretations that partake of some of the hermeneutic potential of the text—cannot distinguish between sacred and secular texts be-

25. *The Genesis of Secrecy: On the Interpretation of Narrative*, 40.

cause the authority that would limit the interpretive field is disseminated by the text itself.

Kermode's discussion relies on Hans-Georg Gadamer's formulation that "the meaning of a text goes beyond its author not sometimes but always"; in the case of the parables under discussion this is true because the text permits the appropriation of its authority when that authority is conceived textually rather than as a function of the "intention" of the author. The parable of the sheep and the goats provides two loci for Christ: one central, transcendent, and authoritative; one dispersed and secularized. In a Blakean reading, the test of righteousness, finally, turns on accepting that Christ occupies the second position, because this choice allows the reader to affirm the unity of humankind without separating the interpreter from that unified body. By giving the reader the attributes of Christ as a man, the Protestant stance of individual interpretation is authorized, inspired by intratextual considerations.

Hence, the reader is moved by the spirit of the text to amend that text but is constrained by it from altering the text. He or she can perform this emendation by linking a new text to the text, through which the text is re-signified. If the result of this process, as Kermode laments, is that sacred texts cannot be separated from secular ones, Blake values this outcome, for he aspires to write the Bible revised to produce the conditions by which we can come to understand our own propensity for oppression, a propensity—as we see in the traditional interpretation of the parable of the sheep and the goats—that emerges even when the avowed purpose of the text is liberatory.

Blake comments on the passage of authority from the traditional exegetical stance that finds a unique and fixed meaning in the Bible to the individual who reads the text and amends it by his or her reading, creating a new "authorized" text: "The Bible or <Peculiar> Word of God, Exclusive of Conscience or the Word of God Universal, is that Abomination which like the Jewish ceremonies is for ever removed & henceforth every man may converse with God & be a King & Priest in his own house" ("Annotations," E615). Here Blake's contempt for the presupposition that any particular text should assume the right of absolute interpretive authority is matched by his enthusiasm for the notion that every person's right to his or her own version of God's Word is itself universal. The ultimate, unassailable authorities of King and Priest are displaced; at the same time, the traditional unitary status of the "Word of God" fragments and serves two distinct functions, analogous to the contradictory status of Blake's own authorship of *Jerusalem* as expressed in the prefatory address. On the one hand, the "Word of God" functions as a foundational concept, providing the link to transcendence and universality. On the other hand, the "Word of God" can be "peculiar"—that is, both individual and odd or *partial*. The "universality" lauded here, therefore, does not refer to the holding of belief in common but rather to the widespread dissemination of the powers of interpretation. As I argue in subsequent sections, Blake's own "peculiar" construction of *Jerusalem* can undermine the institutionalized oppression "peculiar" sacred texts promote insofar as it enables his readers to confront its "fabricated" nature as it proclaims its "originality." Thus, Blake's readers can learn the "sacred" mechanism for appropriating the authority that creates the illusion of universal or determinate meaning in order to *unfix* that meaning, to allow it to circulate.

Bounding Lines

What is at stake in Blake's version of the Higher Criticism? Blake's use of the parable of the sheep and the goats exposes his sophisticated understanding of the means by which textual authority is produced in the biblical texts, situating him in opposition to two apparently different models of interpretive authority. Blake's practice contradicts the traditional hermeneutic view that interpretation consists in recovering the unitary original meaning deposited by God—or by prophets "channeling" God's intention—interpretations validated by institutionally authorized, mediating interpretations. Historically, the alternative to the traditional exegetic stance is represented by the Dissenters' contention that each individual has the ability to perceive God's intention in an unmediated way, by means of an "Inner Light." Even though Blake's revision of the parable of the sheep and the goats to reject the transcendental interpretive authority would seem to position him in this Dissenting camp, his distinction in the address "To the Public" between the source that "dictated" the poem to him and *himself* as source of the poem subverts the concept of immanence on which the Inner Light doctrine depends. The Dissenting view proposes that the individual has a perceptual faculty that grants unmediated access to divine intention and eternal truth, whereas Blake indicates that the individual can learn to perceive the mediations that make perceptions seem not only natural and unmediated but possible at all. In short, Blake's work suggests that the individual does not gain access to a realm of ideality but does learn how to recognize the naturalizing strategies and effects of ideologies.

Blake's criticism of these interpretive models derives from his insistence on two radical positions: first, that there are neither transcendental nor ontologically prior positions from which to authorize interpretations, a claim antithetical to the traditional exegetes as well as to the Dissenters; and second, that all perception is ideologically mediated and ipso facto limited, a claim directed particularly at the Inner Light doctrine. While the Higher Criticism could provide Blake with the tools he needs to expose the interpretive mediations that create the illusion of interpretive validity, Blake does not subscribe to the Higher Criticism's project of establishing a different yet unassailable principle of transcendental authority. Along with some other eighteenth-century thinkers, such as Thomas Paine and David Hume, Blake recognizes that what is held up as a disembodied "transcendental authority" descending from the empyrean to reveal transhistorical truths is actually a function of secular and institutional powers that disguise their own material processes and historical interests. Blake's extension of this insight to affirm that perception *could not take place* without the prior mediation of ideologically constituted interpretations—in effect, that all perception traces the lineaments of its constitutive ideological assumptions—provides the key to Blakean textuality.

Jerusalem has many features that signal Blake's continuing interest in Higher Critical principles, which he encountered in Alexander Geddes's reviews and project to retranslate the Bible. Geddes's *Prospectus of a new translation of the Holy Bible* contains an extended example of the role that ideological motivation plays in the production of the biblical texts. Commenting on the *Masora*, which was *the* authoritative scriptural text for biblical translators before the textual studies of the eighteenth century, Geddes remarks first on the illegitimate assumption of authority by the early translators, an assumption made possible by their rhetorical skills:

> It may, nevertheless, be confidently affirmed, that the greatest part of those who have entered into it [biblical translation] for these last three hundred years, have voluntarily put out their own eyes, and allowed themselves to be led on by the worst of guides. The same imposing set of men, who had the audacity and art to make the Christian world believe that they had preserved the text of their Scriptures in its original integrity, by a pretended enumeration of every word and letter, found it equally easy to perswade them, that the true reading and meaning had also been preserved by the punctuation of every syllable, and the distinction of every pause. This was the second part of that wonderful MASORA, without which the Hebrew text was supposed to be a mere dead letter, a nose of wax, a body without a soul.[26]

Geddes seems most bothered by the unfounded assumption that a mere textual operation can provide the basis for believing that a given interpretation represents the intentions of the text's author. We ought to notice that these stabilizing operations ("a pretended enumeration of every word and letter") echo Blake's assertion at the opening of *Jerusalem* that "Every word and every letter is studied and put into its fit place," because the oscillation of authority that Blake's intervention in the "dictated" text produces has its counterpart in Geddes's discussion of the relationship of the *Masora* to the Hebrew scriptural texts.

By virtue of its claims to "preserve by punctuation . . . the true reading and meaning" of the Hebrew text, this "second part" of the *Masora* assumes priority over the original. Yet it is clear that Geddes understands that there can be no access to an original text. He brings

26. *Prospectus*, 63.

this home to his English reader by reproducing a page of the Masoretic text as it might appear were it written in English. He explains that the original text was written "in one uniform character, and without any of our modern marks of distinction," so he writes

> INTHEBEGINNINGGODCREAT
> EDTHEHEAUENANDTHEEARTH

Then he represents the "Masoretic punctuation" of these lines, after suitable explanation of the meaning of these vowel points with regard to pronunciation, as follows:

> IN THE BEGINNING GOD CREA
> TED THE HEAUEN AND THE EARTH

Geddes proceeds to explain why this elaborate system of punctuation and tonal expression can bear no necessary resemblance to the original text:

> For how are the powers of these very symbols ascertained, but by an immediate appeal to living sounds and the now prevailing modes of utterance? If these happen to change, as we know they imperceptibly do, what will be the use of your boasted symbols at any future period? and by what canons will their respective powers be ascertained? Granting even, that they had, like Ezekiel's mystic wheels, a living and selfinterpretating spirit within them, that could effectually and for ever arrest so fleeting a thing as vocal air; why is their position in the text so awkward and unnatural?[27]

In the face of similar questioning by Louis Cappel, which threatened to overturn the "fundamental article of Protestantism . . . at one blow"—that is, which suggested that the Masoretic punctuation and vowel points did not have a divine origin—church authorities decided to declare that divinity as a canonical article:

> But what could not be done by skill or learning, was done by dint of authority. In the year 1679 a special canon was framed at Ge-

27. Ibid., 64–65.

neva and adopted by all the Helvetian churches; by which it was decreed that no one should in future be admitted to the sacred ministry, who did not publicly acknowledge the Masoretic text to be divine and authentic; both as to *consonants* and *vowels*.[28]

Geddes's explanation of the Geneva canon makes it clear that "divine origin" is a function of interpretation and institutionalized authority; he discloses that the motivation directing this interpretation seeks to occult its own (abuse of) power behind the invocation and invention of another, higher power.

Moreover, Geddes points to a distinction between the text as signifier (consonants, vowels, punctuation, spacing) versus the text as signified; as part of this distinction, he draws attention to the malleability of the signifier/signified relationship, its arbitrary yet conventional nature. Some possibilities for disarticulating conventional meanings from their signifiers by manipulating the signifier itself appear in Geddes's text: "What if other pedagogues . . . had thrown out by degrees, the original vowels, now become useless lumber; and if instead of GOD, HEAVEN, EARTH, you were presented with GD, HVN, ERTH, bespattered with pricks and patches as above? . . . [these] often confuse the mind, as much as they bewilder the eye. . . ."[29] These uncouplings of signifier and signified that result from the distortion of the material level of the text remind us of Blake's own practice. Not only does Blake punctuate *Jerusalem* with examples of the "wall of words"—to use Vincent De Luca's phrase—that Geddes's presentation of the first words of Genesis produces (see Plate 86), but he draws attention to the graphic character of the signifiers that make up his text as well. The innumerable tiny figures, flourishes, twining vines, soaring birds, and various beetles and flying insects—in addition to the prevalence of other indeterminate marks on the page that stud the interlinear spaces of some plates and may or may not serve for punctuation or emphasis—frequently blend with or alter the appearance of a letter or word. As a result, we find ourselves "reading" Blake's graphic productions, concentrating, as Robert Essick puts it, "on the accidents (as distinct from the supposed essence) of language, its surfaces and material

28. Ibid., 67.
29. Ibid., 66.

presences as aural or visual images, and the ways Blake may or may not have exploited that materiality to generate meanings within an alternative semiotics."³⁰

Furthermore, the astounding fact that no two versions of the same work by Blake are alike recalls Geddes's description of the evolution of the Masoretic text:

> And here I cannot help remarking, that the Masoretic punctuation has been productive of the greatest evil, where it has been credulously supposed to be the most productive of good. The real vocal letters, being once stript of their vocal powers and deemed quiescent consonants, were gradually thrown out as useless, or omitted as unnecessary; according to the negligence or caprice of transcribers: for what need is there (they probably said) scrupulously to retain a *vau*, when a *holem* or *kibbutz* performs its functions; or a *jod* when its place is so well supplied by a *hirik-katon*, *tzere* or *segol*? Hence we do not meet with any two manuscripts, that are alike in these particulars; and by far the greatest number of various readings arise from the accidental or intentional omission of those two letters.³¹

This is a different type of indeterminacy than that described by McGann in his discussion of Geddes's "fragment hypothesis," for here the interpretive problem arises from markings on the page that have come to appear arbitrary or accidental rather than from the exclusion, inclusion, or altered order of sections of the text. Geddes evidently believes that a plain meaning could be recovered from the examination of the "original" unpointed text (if an "original" could be found), but, of course, in Blake's case, no such "original" exists.³²

In fact, Blake is at pains to multiply variants, not to suppress them, as Stephen Leo Carr and Robert Essick have demonstrated. Carr explains that the variations in copies of Blake's works differ from those that occur in conventional printmaking: unlike the latter, which "achieve their significance only in and through an economy

---

30. De Luca, "A Wall of Words: The Sublime as Text"; Essick, "How Blake's Body Means," 213. Two other extremely useful works that address the significance of Blake's "graphism" are Nelson Hilton's *Literal Imagination: Blake's Vision of Words* and Stephen Leo Carr's "Illuminated Printing: Toward a Logic of Difference."
31. *Prospectus*, 70.
32. See McGann, "Idea," 2.

of scarcity," Blake's variations "immediately and significantly alter the design: material differences introduced in reproduction themselves produce alternative construals or performances of a page." As a way of contrasting Geddes's and Blake's interest in these variations, we might say that Geddes believes them all to be versions of an original source text, the reconstruction of which is the task of the textual scholars, while Blake's practice emphasizes the proliferation of alternative readings that could emerge if every mark on the page is deemed significant, no matter how accidentally placed or meaningless it first appears. Although Blake and Geddes would then have two separate projects, their descriptions of the text as a material, graphic signifying system and of the process of reading as interpretive production would be consistent.[33]

Essick revises Carr's notion of the function of these "random" marks: "They actively thwart iconicity by disrupting the stability and repeatability basic to the way verbal signs and their visual representatives (letters or iconic images) ideally function . . . [they] affect *how* something is represented and not *what* is represented." In fact, they enact a different kind of representation, one Essick calls "phenomenological and incarnational rather than structural and transcendental"; the first is a type of sign that signifies its materiality and its history of production, whereas the other insists on presenting itself as a mere vehicle for referential meaning. Although the terms are clumsy, they point to two different kinds of engagement with the text. The "incarnational" sign invites multiple readings, enthusiastic play with the text; the "transcendental" sign provokes a decoding.[34]

Essick's sympathies clearly lie with the incarnational sign, and surely he is right to emphasize its importance for current Blake scholarship, particularly in light of the neglect of this dimension of Blake's work. But Essick has his own project of "transcendence." For him, the incarnational sign itself offers a productive analogy to "Blake's sense of the immanence of spirit within the body, for which Christ is the paradigmatic type."[35] If we refer back to the address "To the Public,"

---

33. "Illuminated Printing," 183. The most astonishing demonstration of this proliferation of alternative readings is Donald Ault's *Narrative Unbound*.
34. "How Blake's Body Means," 209 and 213.
35. Ibid., 212.

we can see that this concept of "immanence" has already been deconstructed; if he subscribed to the Inner Light doctrine, Blake would only need to iterate one or the other of the positions he claims for the origin of the poem. However, insofar as Blake's presentation makes these sources at the same time mutually exclusive *and* compatible, it invites us to resist reading his position as analogous to the doctrine of the incarnation and to concentrate instead on the ways in which Blake's textual practice provides opportunities for the reader to confront his or her own tendencies to presume that a reading is true or inevitable when it is in fact a product of occulted interpretive assumptions.

One consequence of understanding textuality as materiality and as a product of motivated interpretations—one consequence, that is, of displacing the referential model of language that undergirds the traditional exegetical stance—is that all appeals to interpretive validity based on immediacy, ontological priority, or access to authorial intention lose authority. For Blake, all reading involves the reader in an encounter with precisely those interpretive assumptions that "guarantee" immediacy, ontological priority, and access to authorial intentions: in effect, Blake sees all reading as the mobilization of precisely those strategies that construct the categories of the natural, the true, and the real in any ideological endeavor. And for Blake, all perception is nothing more than this type of reading: "perception" never serves as a sign of immediacy in Blake, but rather as a sign of textualization, of occulted motivations. Perception is never *prior to* interpretation but always a *function of* interpretation.

If we look at the most famous example of Blake's interest in perceptual relativism—the reading of the sun as heavenly host in "A Vision of The Last Judgment," written in 1810 (that is, in the middle of the period in which Blake was writing *Jerusalem*)—we can begin to understand that Blake thought of the world as a text because he thought of perception as an act of interpretation: "What it will be Questiond When the Sun rises do you not see a round Disk of fire somewhat like a Guinea O no no I see an Innumerable company of the heavenly host crying Holy Holy Holy is the Lord God Almighty I question not my Corporeal or Vegetative Eye any more than I would Question a Window concerning a Sight I look thro it & not with it" ("Vision," E565–66). Northrop Frye has used this quotation to stress the relationship between imagination and reality in Blake's work:

"The Hallelujah-Chorus perception of the sun makes it a far more real sun than the guinea-sun, because more imagination has gone into perceiving it."[36] For Frye, there are two kinds of perception, one dull and unimaginative, which fosters an unreal existence, and another, vividly imaginative, which produces reality. But it takes no less imagination to see the sun as a guinea than as a heavenly host, pace Frye, since it is a virtual commonplace—and therefore relatively unimaginative—to conceive of the sun in mythological terms as a personified divinity.

I would argue that Blake's point might equally well be that most men see the sun in terms of the ideological system that, during the eighteenth century, produced a discourse which was actively engaged in making itself appear natural while disguising its own internal contradictions: the economic discourse. Men see the sun in terms of their economic well-being, a perception which, for the average Englishman, would always appear to be "natural." The writings of Richard Price, himself an intimate of Joseph Priestley, and the writings of other English radicals, such as Paine and Godwin, analyze the fallacies of the arguments supporting property rights and provide a lucidly compelling discussion of the ways in which people are duped into believing that nature supports the contemporary distribution of wealth.[37] Those who interpret the world in terms of money do not believe that they are interpreting at all: they are seeing "what is," the normal state of affairs. To see the forces at work that naturalize ideological constructs, we need only note that

36. *Fearful Symmetry*, 21. In his recent book, *Constructive Vision and Visionary Deconstruction: Los, Eternity, and the Productions of Time in the Later Poetry of William Blake*, Peter Otto also takes Frye to task on this point: Frye's reading, Otto says, "seems to me to miss the point. The perception of the sun as a guinea is tied to the economy of the self. A guinea is something which we can use; it suggests a world that is seen only in terms of its relative usefulness to the self" (12). Although I disagree with Otto's metaphysics throughout the book, I find his insight into Frye's (and other commentators') failure to recognize the ideological purport of the guinea-sun perception refreshing.

37. The writings of Price, Paine, and Godwin were published by Joseph Johnson and reviewed in *The Analytical Review* and therefore likely to have been known by Blake, whose own views on the deadly effects of using money as a standard for all value have been well documented. My intention here, however, is not to demonstrate what Blake thought of the value of money, but rather to show that the example of the guinea-sun is not innocent. Such a perception reveals the prior interference of a specific ideological construction.

Blake scholars have always regarded this delineation of the sun as a coin to be a mere description of its appearance, ignoring Blake's graphic representation of the *O* immediately following "guinea."

All of Blake's diatribes against the senses are related to his criticism of the belief in unmediated perception. Once we grasp that Blake completely rejects the notion that *any* perception can be unmediated, that is, that perception can evade the constitutive forces of ideology, we can understand why Blake says that he *sees* rather than *hears* the crying of the chorus, for here he indicates his view of the world as "text"—the site of the play of interpretations motivated by specific historical forces. If all experience is mediated by interpretive assumptions, it is important to expose those assumptions because they limit our perception, creating the simulation of universality and yoking us to forces just out of sight. We all interpret in closed ways, and the limitations of our interpretations apply to our readings of the world and to the text.

However, precisely because perception is a product of interpretation, an effect of prior assumptions, precisely because no experience is untouched by history or ideology, these same limitations are what make it possible for perception to take place at all. The world, the Bible, the Blakean text—all are produced by acts of interpretation, the motivation of which is more or less obscured. The Higher Criticism exposed the presence of multiple motivations in the construction of the biblical text; Blake's later poems do not simply repeat this exposition but work to analyze the limiting and the productive power of interpretive assumptions, the productive power that *arises* from those very limitations.

Yet the most radical component of Blake's view is not the deconstruction of perception that it implies, not its exposure of the false promise of immediacy and validity that our uncritical concept of "perception" betokens, but rather its absolute refusal to propose an alternative route to truth. The disclosure of perception as interpretation does not signify a loss or a mistake that has to be rectified. Blake is not saying to us that we have been looking for truth in the wrong ways or in the wrong places; he is saying that we have been blind to the ways in which we construct "truths" that oppress us. When I read a Blakean text, I do not find counter truths that correct my erroneous thinking, but I do meet at every turn my own rage for determinacy, my own strategies for rigidifying what is inherently fluid, my own need to impose order and to dominate, my own desire for the very transcendent guarantees that legitimate tyrannies. Most importantly, however, I learn that I cannot read, cannot perceive, cannot conceive my own subjectivity *without* precisely those desires, those practices, those strategies. To be human, I must produce and devour the text, the world, myself, again and again.

These interpretive assumptions, these ideologically *given* categories and structures, both constrain and energize, like the "bounding lines" of Blake's 1809 *Descriptive Catalog:*

> The great and golden rule of art, as well as of life, is this: That the more distinct, sharp, and wirey the bounding line, the more perfect the work of art; and the less keen and sharp, the greater is the evidence of weak imitation, plagiarism, and bungling. . . . The want of this determinate and bounding form evidences the want of idea in the artist's mind, and the pretence of the plagiary in all its branches. How do we distinguish the oak from the beech, the horse from the ox, but by the bounding outline? How do we distinguish one face or countenance from another, but by the bounding line and its infinite inflexions and movements? What is it that builds a house and plants a garden, but the definite and determinate? What is it that distinguishes honesty from knavery, but the hard and wirey line of rectitude and certainty in the actions and intentions. Leave out this l[i]ne and you leave out life itself; all is chaos again, and the line of the almighty must be drawn out upon it before man or beast can exist. (E550)

It is possible to argue that Blake is demanding representational veracity in this passage, a normative reproduction of oak and beech, horse and ox. But the conclusion suggests a more complex vision. The omission of the *i* in "Leave out this l[i]ne" recapitulates in its form what the phrase asserts: that the I/eye—the material, historical, individual point from which one views—is constitutive of the order of the world and therefore the equivalent of the (lower-case) "almighty." On this reading, the conditions that create the "line of the almighty" are neither fixed ("its infinite flexions and movements") nor transcendental; rather they are temporal, contingent, determinately particular. The "weak imitation" is contemptible not because it is a copy, but because it betrays itself by its lack of limitation and particularity.[38] The biblical reference to the production and disruption of "chaos" as a recurring process—as well as the use of the passive voice in "the line of the almighty must be drawn again"—indicates that Blake once again uncouples a unitary, absolute, and temporally prior concept of origin from his concept of artistic authorship.

Although in another philosophical context "particularity" might correspond to "immediacy," it is clear that for Blake all particularity is *produced*, mediated by "actions and intentions." The bounding lines are both the manifestation and the cause of those "intentions." They make intention perceptible and determinate. In art, bounding lines do not reproduce an unmediated perception of "things as they are," but the way in which individual artists see things. Bounding lines do not guarantee that the manifestation of intentions is "absolutely true," but they do trace, accurately, the effects of "motivation"; they are "honest" in delineating the bounds of interest and the mediations governing perception. The bounding line functions like the "peculiar Word of God" insofar as it produces an embodiment, manifests a particular interest or partiality, and consequently identifies itself as individual.

By attending to the material signifiers of Blake's text, not as doors to the experience of the "immanence of the spirit" but as sites provoking interpretive limitation, the reader encounters the act of perception in its double nature: on the one hand as an experience of the already interpreted, where the hegemonically determined nature of perception is revealed as such; and on the other hand, and at the same time, as an experience of the pressure-to-interpret provoked by the excess of potentiality of meaning that is the paradoxical but direct result of the apparently passive and arbitrary character of perception. Each of the signifiers, the marks on Blake's pages, then, can serve as a bounding line: we will always see it *as* something and we can see as well that *what* it seems to be shifts in order to meet our own desire for determinacy. These marks provide occasions for us

---

38. Janet Warner's engrossing book on the visual languages of Blake's era, *Blake and the Language of Art*, confirms that Blake had no quarrel with copying as an artistic, creative mode; imitation of previous artists provides access to a visual language, but every artist has to develop a unique grammar and respect the capacity of the images to establish new significations in different contexts. See her conclusion, 185–86ff.; see also David Bindman's "Blake's Theory and Practice of Imitation."

to uncover our own motivated interpretations in the "perception" of the text, openings for us to re-mark our implication in ideological dissemination, and opportunities for us to work some transformations on those limitations.

Re-Citing "The Bard": Natural Language, Referentiality, and the Possessive Selfhood

*B*ecause all perception involves an occulted act of interpretation, a poem that calls into question a reader's strategies for imposing determinate interpretations could help reeducate that reader into a profoundly different relationship to the world. By undermining the position of the author as the origin of the text, by making the source of the poem both internal and external to itself, by refusing to provide a stable contextual determinant, and by indicating the pernicious effects of such determinacy, Blake encourages the reader to confront the ways in which he or she uses such contexts (such as the idea of author-as-origin) to create "authoritative" interpretations. In fact, Blake compels the reader to recognize both the necessity for and the artificial and unstable existence of these contexts in the production of any meaning.

According to poststructuralist theory, language can mean at all only if it can be separated from an original determinate context: we produce the meaning of words not by finding the source of meaning but by appropriating them to new contexts—our own. The "readability" of a text depends not only upon its association with a definite context or consciousness but also upon its *dissociation* from a determinate context or consciousness. It requires the disruption of context—from a particular reader, a particular point of view, a particular author—so that other contexts, other readers, other "writers," may employ it. The possibility that language will escape the intention of its author, that the text will free itself from its supposed referent, that the poem works to sever itself from a determinate context, is fundamentally the way that language is able to "mean," because language is composed of signifying forms, recognizable as such, without the imposition of conditions of intention. This is what makes it possible for us to appropriate the signifying forms of language for our own uses, although those language events necessarily carry with them the potential for their being used or understood in ways not under our control. Given that every signifying form can be put in quotation marks (cited), it can break with every given context, as Derrida explains, "engendering an infinity of new contexts in a manner which is absolutely illimitable. . . . This does not imply that the mark is valid outside of a context, but on the contrary, that there are only contexts without any center or absolute anchoring."[39] The text that cites itself, as *Jerusalem* does in its final signature, "The Song of Jerusalem," disrupts its own original or teleological context, bringing to the surface the freedom inherent to make language meaningful by contextual displacement.

The poem anticipates the formalist objection that such an approach relegates the text to a jumble of senseless signs. As Derrida formulates it, all signifying forms achieve their validity within a context, and in the commentary on Chaos at the end of the poem—in the eternity of "readability" described in those closing plates—Chaos is rescued from meaninglessness by the renewed and continuous production of meanings through the creation of different contexts. Thus "the dim Chaos brightend beneath above around! Eyed as the Peacock / According to the Human Nerves of Sensation" (Plate 98). Here we see the power of multiple viewpoints, derived from the "Expansion and Contraction [of] . . . the Organs of Perception":

> And every Man stood Fourfold. each Four Faces had. One to the West
> One toward the East One to the South One/ to the North. the Horses Fourfold
> And the dim Chaos brightend beneath, above around! Eyed as the Peacock

39. "Signature Event Context," 186.

> According to the Human Nerves of Sensation. the Four Rivers
>   of the Water of Life
> South stood the Nerves of the Eye. East in Rivers of bliss the
>   Nerves of the
> Expansive Nostrils West. flowd the Parent Sense the Tongue.
>   North stood
> The labyrinthine Ear . . .
> And the Four Faces of Humanity fronting the Four Cardinal
>   Points
> Of Heaven going forward irresistible from Eternity to Eternity
> And they conversed together in Visionary forms dramatic
>   which bright
> Redounded from their Tongues in thunderous majesty, in
>   Visions
> In new Expanses, creating exemplars of Memory and of
>   Intellect
> Creating Space, Creating Time according to the wonders Divine
> Of Human Imagination, throughout all the Three Regions
>   immense
> Of Childhood, Manhood & Old Age & the all tremendous un-
>   fathomable Non Ens
> Of Death was seen in regenerations terrific or complacent
>   varying
> According to the subject of discourse & every Word & Every
>   Character
> Was Human according to the Expansion or Contraction, the
>   Translucence or
> Opakeness of Nervous fibres such was the variation of Time &
>   Space
> Which vary according as the Organs of Perception vary & they
>   walked
> To & fro in Eternity as One Man reflecting each in each &
>   clearly seen
> And seeing: according to fitness and order.
>   (Plate 98)

As one example of the productiveness of contextual shifts in these lines, we can note that the punctuation and line breaks of

> South stood the Nerves of the Eye. East in Rivers of bliss the
>   Nerves of the
> Expansive Nostrils West. flowd the Parent Sense the Tongue.
>   North stood
> The labyrinthine Ear . . .

subvert any attempt to ascribe definitively one direction to one sense. These contextual shifts bring shifts in consciousness and transform perception, but they are not dominated by a single aim or origin. The "constant" in these closing plates is the continually transforming and transformative text/context of *Jerusalem*, not some essence that pervades all things nor a determinate origin. Without a multiplicity of viewpoints and contexts, there is no possibility of significance.

In the absence of contextual rupture, writing becomes a kind of bondage, a "spectrous oath," linking word and object in an absolute symmetry. The interpretive strategy that insists on equating the origin and the meaning of the text is the same strategy that insists on the denotative nature of language, nature as referent. But this founding origin, whether in nature or in consciousness, can never appear anywhere as absolutely present. It can only be figured in a series of substitutions.[40] In the final plates of *Jerusalem*, the contextual rupturing that founds the signifying process presents itself as a tropological function—the metonymic displacement of contexts. Plate 94, which begins the process of Albion's awakening and thus serves as the climax of the poem, institutes a dramatic figuration of metonymic displacement. Each displacement results in an "awakening" and the appearance of a new subject. At the same time, these individual metonymic displacements are successively gathered together into ever larger contexts: "England who is Brittannia enterd Albions bosom rejoicing . . . So spake the Vision of Albion & in him so spake in my hearing / The Universal Father" (Plates 96–97).

Each "awakening" makes language possible—this is the moment of "readability," the rupturing from a determinate context that permits signification: "And England who is Brittannia awoke from Death on Albions bosom . . . her voice pierc'd Albions clay cold ear. he moved upon the Rock / The Breath Divine went forth" (Plates 94–95). The rupture is followed by the conferring of a name, a designa-

---

40. In *Of Grammatology*, Derrida explains: "There has never been anything but writing; there have never been anything but supplements, substitutive significations which could only come forth in a chain of differential references, the 'real' supervening, and being added only while taking on meaning from a trace and from an invocation of the supplement, etc. And thus to infinity, for we have read, *in the text*, that the absolute present [and] Nature . . . have always escaped, have never existed; that what opens meaning and language is writing as the disappearance of natural presence" (159).

tion of a new context, which functions as a substitution or a metaphor for the subject until the next rupture occurs. England becomes Brittannia and in so doing awakens Albion; at this point Albion becomes the sun which in turn reveals Jesus, who then appears in a simile as Los.

The conferring of the name—the establishing of the meaning-as-identity—then, involves two modes of language. First, it functions as a mark of identity, of what is proper to the subject. This is the first step in the regeneration of a "determinate" meaning after the contextual rupture. Although it is necessary for purposes of explication to describe this as a chronological process, neither step is logically prior. This first mode corresponds to the one-to-one designation of absolute reference so often marked in Blake's text by the activity of the Spectre of Reason, the "oath" or "law." This referential moment, however, is absolutely necessary for signification to appear, because it provides the element of sameness, of presence, on which signification depends. We can recognize that this is language seen in what Paul Ricoeur calls its "hermeneutic function"—its referential or denotative aspect—which requires a phenomenal here and now, a fixed point of view, a definite origin that governs the relationship between sign and referent.[41]

The second mode of language concerns its tropological or rhetorical function: Blake refigures the referential moment as a trope, a substitution by metaphor or simile. A name is already a metaphor, a turning away from identity as inherent; it consequently inscribes the possibility/necessity of difference or contextual definition. The pun "enterd/interred" remarks the passage from identity to difference, from one context to another. The rhetorical figure, then, functions as the sign of contextuality. Ricoeur says that we have recourse to the rhetorical function when the "original" authority appears as textually or rhetorically constituted. This rhetorical moment in the text, the stabilizing by a troping that is itself unstable, calls attention to the renewed possibility for contextual rupture, and the process begins again. By the end of the poem, Blake writes this continual movement of the figures, this continual troping, as producing *Jerusalem* itself. When the poem advises us of "the Name of their ema-

---

41. See Ricoeur, "What Is a Text?," 148–49.

Natural Language, Referentiality, and the Possessive Selfhood 53

nations they are named Jerusalem," the emanations stand in for the contextual rupturing/troping that liberates us from the oppressive effects of denotative referential naming, and the sign of their necessary supplement to the process of signification is revealed in the reversed "n-a-m-e" that begins "e-m-a-n-ations."[42]

Plate 94 marks a turning point in the narrative and an interpretive crux. This plate instigates the series of metonymic substitutions that move us from Albion's deathlike trance to his fourfold form, but the *cause* of the transition is elided in the narrative:

> Albion cold lays on his Rock . . .
> The weeds of Death inwrap his hands & feet blown incessant . . .
> And the Body of Albion was closed apart from all Nations.
> Over them the famishd Eagle screams on boney Wings and around
> Them howls the Wolf of famine deep heaves the Ocean black thundering
> Around the wormy Garments of Albion: then pausing in deathlike silence
> Time was Finished! The Breath Divine Breathed over Albion
> . . . And England who is Brittannia awoke from Death on Albions bosom

This account represents its own lack of narrative causality by inserting the screaming eagle, howling wolf, and thundering ocean, entities whose meaningless sounds effect the ultimate rupture of "deathlike silence." Importantly, the text re-marks this rupture by means of an intertextual allusion to Gray's "The Bard," a poem which *also* comments upon the interplay of referential and contextual signification.

According to Gray, "The Bard" reproduces the curse pronounced by the last Welsh bard on Edward the First in retaliation for Edward's execution of the Welsh poets. That is, the poem itself is a kind of citational rupture concerned with a destruction of meaningful language. The Bard bemoans the loss of nature's voice that followed the murders:

---

42. To my knowledge, Nelson Hilton was the first to remark on the inversion of "name" in "emanation." See his *Literal Imagination*. Thomas Vogler's "Re:Naming *MIL/TON*" contains an extended, fascinating discussion of the significance of naming and the function of the emanations in Blake's later work.

> 'Hark, how each giant-oak, and desert cave,
> 'Sighs to the torrent's awful voice beneath!
> '. . . Vocal no more, since Cambria's fatal day,
> 'To high-born Joel's harp, or soft Llewellyn's lay
> (ll. 23–28)

The death of the poets renders nature's voice unintelligible, but the last bard is unable to change this situation until the dead poets reappear. The conditions preceding their return are these:

> 'Far, far aloof th'affrighted ravens sail;
> 'The famished eagle screams, and passes by.
> 'Dear lost companions of my tuneful art,
> 'Dear, as the light that visits these sad eyes,
> 'Dear, as the ruddy drops that warm my heart,
> 'Ye died amidst your dying country's cries—
> 'No more I weep. They do not sleep.
> 'On yonder cliffs, a grisly band,
> 'I see them sit.
> (ll. 37–45)

Upon their resurrection, they join the Bard "in dreadful harmony . . . And weave with bloody hands the tissue of [Edward's] line" (ll. 47–48). The effectiveness of the curse as a prophecy of Edward's demise depends upon the multiplicity of voices, the conjoining of prior texts. Here, as in the climax of *Jerusalem*, "the famished eagle" screams before a resurrection, a new temporality, a transfiguration, and a renewed access to signifying power.[43]

> 43. The second phrase of the crux of Plate 94—"and around / Them howls the Wolf of famine"—may also be related to another poem, book 4 of William Cowper's "The Task." Blake's admiration of Cowper's work is well known, and echoes of the poem can found throughout *Jerusalem:* Blake explicitly refers to the writing of his poem as his "great task!" in Plate 5. The section of book 4 that seems most relevant concerns Cowper's desire to represent the world of language that he finds inadequately portrayed in his newspaper:
>
>> . . . The great debate
>> The popular harangue, the tart reply,
>> The logic, and the wisdom, and the wit,
>> And the loud laugh—I long to know them all;
>> I burn to set th'imprisoned wranglers free,
>> And give them voice and utterance once again.
>> (ll. 30–35)

However, in Gray's poem the loss of "natural" language marks the crisis. The Bard needs "natural" language to prophesy the actual destruction of Edward and his (un)natural descendants of his union with the "she-wolf of France." Consequently, the Bard privileges the referential power of language, its presentation of itself as a natural sign, a sign that "erases" its own tropological aspect. In Gray's poem and in Blake's, the screaming of the eagle signifies the breaking of the link between sign and (natural) referent, subverting na-

---

The loss of living presence, of signifying power, that Cowper remarks on here parallels Gray's concerns in "The Bard." In the following lines, Cowper establishes a universal viewpoint, detached from "the globe and its concerns, I seem advanced / To some secure and more than mortal height, / That liberates and exempts me from them all" (ll. 95–97). His shift from a phenomenalistic, limited point of view to a transcendent vantage allows him to become like God, able to survey "the great Babel" of the world that "turns submitted to my view, turns round / With all its generations" (ll. 98–99). At this point, Cowper remarks upon the fallen condition of the world, the decline of man from human to animal state and the subsequent loss of meaningful language:

> . . . I mourn the pride
> And avarice that make man a wolf to man;
> Hear the faint echo of those brazen throats
> By which he speaks the language of his heart.
> (ll. 102–5)

These lines recall one reading of the opening of *Jerusalem* in which Albion's pride makes him reject the Saviour's voice, calling "man an enemy to man." Cowper describes the language of his world, the modern Babel, as represented in the medium of his newspaper as

> cataracts of declamation thunder here;
> There forests of no meaning spread the page,
> In which all comprehension wanders, lost"
> (ll. 73–75).

If the line "the famish'd eagle screams" signifies the loss of "natural language" in Gray and Blake, so may the howling wolf, whose association to famine may be prefigured here in "brazen throats," and the thundering ocean achieve part of their significance by reference to Cowper's commitment to reestablish poetry in a world where meaning has been rejected. Cowper feels himself "Fast bound in chains of silence," a silence Blake resignifies as a citational rupture. However, Cowper's solution, the turn to the "living" voice and the language of emotion, does not eradicate the conditions of limitation that arise from the phenomenalistic orientation of the subject, its absolute reference to its physical self. Albion, on this view then, would be an example of what Cowper seeks to reject and the logical outcome of Cowper's solution.

ture as a determinate context. In "The Bard," however, the break occasions despair; in Blake's poem, the rupture creates the conditions for transfiguration.

Among other things, Albion's stony sleep is a figure for the domination of just that referential aspect of language, the priority of the centralized subject as determining its "property" and fixing the identity of its objects. In his first speech of Plate 4, Albion is unaware of the rhetorical function of his own self-proclaimed denotative discourse; in his condemnation of the "simulative" character of the voice's speech, Albion establishes himself, his intention, and his property as the total context within which language is to function. Blake signals Albion's refusal of tropological power with a trope: Albion "away turns," he is a-verse, without trope. The attempted repression of the tropological aspect of language results in the elevation of denotation and referentiality to the status of "law."

As I argue in the next section, Albion's own language, however, slips out from under this repressive dictate: he has "jealous fears"—fears of being displaced—which are confirmed by the voice's imprecation to lose its identity and become "One" with a multitude of others. Yet Albion must himself rely upon tropes, metonymically refiguring the source of that voice as a "phantom of the over heated brain" and a "shadow." Thus Albion reproduces the "simulative" properties of the previous speech, employing a rhetoric of similitude that permits metonymic displacement at the very moment that he seeks to disallow it. Blake reminds the reader of this recourse to tropology by the word *dissembling*. Once the reader sees the interdependence of referentiality and rhetoricity in the production of meaning, Albion's speech appears as a kind of reflection or incorporation of the speech he tries to negate. Each implies the other.

In Gray's poem we also find that troping makes referentiality possible and gives it a provisional stability. At the moment that language achieves its fullest power in the poem—the power of the prophetic curse—the poetic voices create a metonymy in the metaphorical "weaving" of the "line." Here too Gray provides Blake with the figure for the metonymic substitution that makes Albion appear in his fourfold guise in Plates 96 and following. The Bard taunts Edward and then throws himself from the cliff into "endless night," dying in order to "triumph":

Natural Language, Referentiality, and the Possessive Selfhood   57

> 'Fond, impious man, think'st thou yon sanguine cloud,
> 'Raised by thy breath, has quenched the orb of day?
> 'To-morrow he repairs the golden flood,
> 'And warms the nations with redoubled ray.
> 'Enough for me: with joy I see
> 'The different dooms our fate assign.
> 'Be thine despair, and sceptered care,
> 'To triumph and to die are mine.'
> He spoke and headlong from the mountain's height
> Deep in the roaring tide he plunged to endless night.
>
> (ll. 135–44)

The Bard proposes as his substitute the figure of the sun who "repairs the golden flood, / And warms the nations with redoubled ray." In Plate 96, Albion also sacrifices himself, throwing himself into the "Furnaces of Affliction," but he has already appeared in Plate 95 as the fulfillment of the Bard's sacrifice, as the figure of the sun who arises from the "endless night" of his "stony sleep." Albion's reawakening as the sun parallels the Bard's vision. Blake even puns on Gray's "redoubled ray," for Albion and his Bow are fourfold, re-doubled. The cloud, the gold flood, the nations of the earth, and the mountain all appear in the climax of *Jerusalem* through the regeneration of Edward's "sanguine breath" as the Breath Divine, an analogue for the rhetorical power of language:

> . . . Albion rose
> In anger: the wrath of God breaking bright flaming on all sides
>   around
> . . . Thou seest the Sun in heavy clouds
> Struggling to rise above the Mountains. in his burning hand
> He takes his Bow, then chooses out his arrows of flaming gold
> Murmuring the Bowstring breathes with ardor! clouds roll
>   around the
> Horns of the wide Bow, loud sounding winds sport on the
>   mountain brows
> . . . the Cloud overshadowing divided them asunder
> . . . So Albion spoke & threw himself into the Furnaces of affliction
> All was a Vision, all a Dream: the Furnaces became
> Fountains of Living Waters flowing from the Humanity Divine
> And all the Cities of Albion rose from their Slumbers, . . .
> . . . Then Albion stood before Jesus in the Clouds
> Of Heaven Fourfold among the Visions of God in Eternity
>
> (Plates 95–96)

Here the movement of the allusion, begun by the scream of the eagle, which both linked and divided Blake's and Gray's texts, has transfigured the rhetorical figures of the "The Bard," figures which project the necessity of their transfiguration as a condition of efficacy or significance. Blake uses the oppositional categories established by Gray's poem, but he doesn't employ Gray's negations: these oppositional categories are regenerated in a new signification.

Blake's presentation of Albion's production of referentiality as a function of his possessive subjectivity effects another intertextual link, for his "demonstrative" credo echoes and transforms the text of Jesus' temptation in the wilderness. We can see the relevance of this allusion easily by focusing upon the function of citation—as a contextual rupture that calls for a determinacy that can only be given tropologically—in the text of the New Testament itself. The history of biblical commentary itself testifies that the tracing of citations and allusions can have no end. All writing is already a "citation." At this juncture, I am concerned with the way in which the citation in the text functions as a sign of intertextuality, rather than simply meaning the content (*énoncé*) of the quotation itself. Antoine Compagnon has described the citation as "a trivial operator of intertextuality" (un opérateur trivial d'intertextualité.) The material contained in the citation "has no meaning outside of the force which effects it, siezes it, exploits it, and incorporates it" (n'a pas de sens hors de la force qui l'agit, qui la saisit, l'exploite et l'incorpore.) This force, seizure, and incorporation are all part of the contextual (dis)articulation that produces meaning. The citation, then, is the paradigmatic case—the most obvious case—of reading as contextual displacement. It is clear that in the act of citing, the subject of the enunciation becomes displaced, with the result being that writing viewed as citational appears without recourse to one single, originating intention. Compagnon says that "in one sense, there is only a subject of citation in a democratic regime of writing" (en un sense, il n'y a de sujet de la citation qu'en régime démocratique de l'écriture.)[44]

An obvious citational interplay occurs in the first exchange between the voice(s) of the "Saviour" and the voice(s) of "Albion" in Plate 4, an exchange which echoes the temptation in the wilderness

---

44. *La seconde main ou le travail de la citation*, 44, 38, and 39. My translations.

Natural Language, Referentiality, and the Possessive Selfhood   59

described in Matthew: here the democratizing effect of contextual displacement emerges as a function of a destabilizing of authority that is already thematized in the biblical text. When Jesus is offered the option of satisfying his hunger by turning stones into bread, he answers Satan: "It is written, Man shall not live by bread alone, but by every word that proceedeth out of the mouth of God" (Matt. 4:4). Unlike Albion, who organizes the world by reference to his sensory limitations, motivated by "jealous fears" that limit his perception of available contexts for producing meaning, Jesus refuses to assert the priority of his self, his hunger, as motivation or origin. Jesus will not produce a univocal, tyrannical relationship between word and thing, between self and world. The life of the self that asserts referentiality as the only principle of language is no life at all, according to the biblical Jesus. Instead, Jesus performs the transformation of stone into bread through a trope, referring to "bread" that does not exist in the phenomenal world except *in potentia*, in his power to transfigure the stones tropologically. Bread and stones are equivalent in their inability to satisfy and in their availability for rhetorical transfiguration, and they are metaphorically identical in Jesus' discourse, which posits another principle by which meaning emerges—the power of signification that derives from recontextualization. "Every word that proceedeth out of the mouth of God" is an allusion to Moses' exhortation to the Israelites to remember how God provided for them in the wilderness: "And he humbled thee, and suffered thee to hunger, and fed thee with manna, which thou knewest not, neither did thy fathers know; that he might make thee know that man doth not live by bread only, but by every *word* that proceedeth out of the mouth of the LORD doth man live" (Deut. 8:3).

Jesus' reference to the Mosaic text seems to reject the possessive self as the definitive context for meaningful language/existence in favor of another ultimate determinant—God. Satan's second temptation makes it clear that he, at least, interprets Jesus' allusion as privileging a hermeneutic view of language in a defensive attempt to provide a unique origin that governs meaning: the Word of God as "it is written" in the Scriptures, Satan reasons, must have the same meaning and power, no matter what the scriptural context. The Scriptures, therefore, are to be read univocally rather than figuratively—or hermeneutically rather than tropologically. This conclusion encourages Satan to quote another text from the Scriptures as his authority for tempting Jesus to throw himself from the pinnacle of the temple. In so doing, Satan displaces Jesus, moving him from wilderness to city, providing a new context for his actions. Jesus, however, follows this rhetorical strategy and performs the same contextual displacement in the scriptural text itself, citing a countertext and thereby undermining the univocity of the Scriptures, opening up a gap between God's word as origin and God's word as intention in order to emphasize the rhetorical rather than the hermeneutical foundation of interpretation.

For the biblical Jesus, the Scriptures are not a univocal text that can be applied, or referred to, with the same result in every situation or context. Instead, he sees it as a collection of tropological maneuvers that allow referentiality to appear as an *effect*. Jesus' troping does not privilege referentiality, but it does produce a designation of the tempter as "Satan." The name—which we are accustomed to regard as denotative—appears out of a tropological moment in the text, a moment that is represented in the text in the action Jesus proposes, the "turn" of "Get thee behind me" (Luke 4:8). Furthermore, the entire process by which names emerge from tropological gestures that efface themselves in a simulation of grounded referentiality appears in this text as a recontextualization of its predecessor text in Deuteronomy.

In the predecessor text, Moses chastises the Israelites for complaining of hunger when they are receiving the Law. Moses explains that God sent manna in place of bread—an entirely new creation, a substitution of which they had never before conceived—in order to make them familiar with the tropes by which meaning emerges, "that he might make thee know that man doth not live by bread only, but by every word that proceedeth out of the mouth of the LORD doth man live" (Deut. 8:3). The literal manna, therefore, stands in for bread, but it also figures what it literally is not, the Word of God. Moses' text sets up a dominating referential principle—the Word of God—which governs the meaning of every thing in the world. Yet that principle appears in a figurative moment in the text. Thus, when Moses produces the commandments, the "Moral Law" that Albion builds and Blake condemns, he is binding language into its referential function by means of figuration.

Natural Language, Referentiality, and the Possessive Selfhood 61

Here the reader is faced with a complex intertextuality that speaks to the issue of authorizing interpretation by reference to a "stable" referential system or a transcendent subjectivity. Albion, unlike Moses and Jesus, displaces the Word of God with his own Selfhood but in order to achieve this position of centrality he must at the same time rely upon the primacy of those predecessor texts and their rhetorical strategies. Blake does not, then, criticize Albion on grounds of impiety nor even on the grounds of his preference for demonstration over faith; rather, he provides the reader with an opportunity to see that the illusion of referentiality is *created* rhetorically. Blake uses these allusions to criticize the reader's reliance upon *any* determinate grounding for meaning, whether divine or natural, while demonstrating the function of context in the genesis of meaning.

In any event, the act of reading the text itself requires that readers become authors who do not stand in an "originary" position vis-à-vis their own texts because the texts are always constructed out of the (dis)articulation of other texts/contexts. Ricoeur comments that "by any supposition reading is a linking together of a new discourse to the discourse of the text," and my point is that, for Blake, the meaningfulness of his linking/writing does not emerge by recourse to the intention of the author nor to the "natural" sign but rather by the rhetorical construction of authority and the stabilizing/destabilizing effects of tropological play.[45] The most important corollary to this conclusion for Blake scholarship is that the Blakean analysis of referentiality and its construction (denotation, "natural language," and so forth) shows that it requires a metaphysical moment equally well represented by the pretensions and aspirations of the possessive or centralized subject and by the universalized vantage point of God.

---

45. "What Is a Text?" 144.

PART TWO

The Subject of Discourse

The Fall from Hermeneutics and the Rhetoric of Subjectivity

The radical potential of Blake's Higher Criticism—as well as the characteristic gestures of Blake's revisionary strategies—emerges in a comparison of his practice with the explicit dictates of the Augustinian hermeneutic. Although Blake concurs with the Augustinian description of the difficulties for biblical (and by extension, all other) interpretation caused by the shifting nature of signification, he reveals with astonishing force the deleterious effects of a reliance on transcendental authority as a solution to those difficulties. In the Blakean revision of the traditional exegetical teachings, the Augustinian importation of a transcendental signifier to stabilize this always unstable interpretive situation is shown to be unfounded and ideologically motivated. In short, Blake's practice is Augustine's without God.

Blake's work responds to several well-known features of the Augustinian method: the acknowledgment that although rhetoric is a "fallen" use of language, that use is necessary in order to interpret the Bible's message of charity and to instruct the Christian reader; the outright assertion that some external or transcendent authority must be invoked so as to make interpretations of the Bible conform to an already decided upon message; the stricture that the Bible cannot be interpreted properly without prior instruction in the requisite method for "producing" God's charitable message; the description of explicit tropological strategies for transforming uncharitable scriptural passages into passages conforming to (what the authorities have decided is) God's message; the analysis of the temporal world as constituted by mediated perceptions transmitted linguistically and an affirmation that words are material entities with material effects; and the theological claim that "evil" is not in itself a substance—because nothing in God's universe can be evil—but rather appears substantial to an observer who has failed to situate a phenomenon properly, that is, with other "like" things.[1]

1. Almost every Blake commentator invokes Augustine at some point, although no scholarship demonstrates Blake's explicit knowledge of Augustine. I think there is abundant textual evidence that Blake knew the *Confessions* and

As I discuss below, each of these elements of Augustinian exegesis has a counterpart in Blakean practice that affirms (or even extends) the implications of the Augustinian analysis while subverting its metaphysics. For example, Blake makes use of the traditional exegetical reliance on the transformative powers of the rhetorical tropes, but he does not apply them in the service of an already determined interpretation. Augustine employs tropes to create the illusion of an a priori, fixed meaning: in *On Christian Doctrine* Augustine agrees that tropes can generate both difference and identity, but he exhorts his readers to employ them in the service of identity alone.[2] Augustine recommends the discovery of the true meaning of an apparently uncharitable figurative expression by recourse to *similitude*, for the "words of which it is composed will be seen to be derived from similar things or related to such things by some association." However, he immediately cautions the reader that "since things are similar to other things in a great many ways, we must not think it to be prescribed that what a thing signifies by similitude in one place must always be signified by that thing." Augustine points directly to the double nature of the tropes of similitude: in some cases, similitude produces an equivalence of identity, but that identity may be unstable. Consequently, similitude can link even extreme opposites. For example, when Augustine is considering those scriptural texts in which two instances of a word have opposite figurative translations—one signifying an instruction to virtue, the other to vice—he advises the use of irony and antiphrasis, which "imply the opposite of what is said." Recourse to these tropes gives Augustine the power to accommodate any text to a single message, no matter how great its apparent distance from his intended interpretation. Thus, irony and antiphrasis function as tropes of identity, for they ultimately assert the equivalence of multiple, apparently incommensurable read-

---

De Doctrina Christiana, even though *De Doctrina* was not published in English until after Blake's death. However, my present argument does not depend upon Blake's familiarity with those texts: scholars agree that Blake knew the general features of the Augustinian hermeneutic, which is sufficient for my claims here.

The passages in Augustine's work that elaborate the features I have outlined can be found primarily in books 1, 2, 5, and 10 of the *Confessions* and book 3 of D. W. Robertson, Jr.'s, translation of *De Doctrina Christiana, On Christian Doctrine* (1958).

2. See especially *On Christian Doctrine*, book 3.xxv–xxix.

ings. Of course, the double articulation of the tropes remains; by refusing to employ the strategies of stabilization on which Augustine relies, Blake can retain the potential of tropes for remarking difference rather than identity. Blake uses the full range of tropological (dis)articulations to disseminate interpretive authority and multiply interpretive possibilities.

Furthermore, Augustine consistently resorts to a transcendental signifier to block interpretive play, whereas Blake just as consistently undermines the authority of such signifiers even as he invites the reader to rely on them. Augustine traces a career from rhetorician to hermeneutician, but Blake exposes and undermines the hidden assumptions of hermeneutics in order to position a tropological or rhetorical praxis in its place. Augustine believed that his conversion removed him from the temporal, fallen, and power-seeking use of language to the revelation of the divinely authorized Word. Blake's journey from hermeneutician to rhetorician amounts to the rejection of a transcendent position from which meaning derives and truth can be guaranteed. At the same time, Blake's work demonstrates that much of the power of rhetoric derives from its capacity to foster the impression that such authority exists.

Blake could find in Augustinian hermeneutics the procedures for generating a "unified" interpretation; he could find as well the proposition that the proper interpretation of scriptural language requires the reader's active transformation of significance and of self. Although their goals differ, insofar as the Augustinian method insists on teleology and ultimate authority while Blakean praxis encourages the dissemination of authority and interpretations, Augustine's analysis of the rhetorical nature of scriptural language and authority could provide Blake with a comprehensive outline of hegemonic linguistic strategies for the production of subjectivity. Augustine's positing of the "givenness" of God's message puts tropological play in the service of a closed hermeneutic: the text must always be made to say what we "know" God meant it to say. When the authority of an a priori hermeneutical touchstone is rejected, as it is in Blake's work, the Augustinian rhetoric can be regenerated for other purposes. The repudiation of fallen language, on account of its ability to enchain men to error through tradition, convention, and rhetorical power, which traditional exegesis emphasizes, provides a key to understanding Blakean practice: just as Augustine has to rely on precisely those capacities of fallen language in order to establish the possibility of an ultimate authority and to transform his audience into "Christian" subjects, so Blake acknowledges the important role that rhetorical, tropological transfigurations have to play in the production and subversion of the conditions of human oppression.

I want to point my readers to two conclusions I will be drawing from Blake's revision of traditional hermeneutics. First, in a Blakean account, the Augustinian method is the exegetical counterpart to all hegemonic practices, practices that foster alienation, misery, and tyranny. Second, and crucially, implicit in Blakean textuality is the realization that such practices are absolutely necessary—for perception, for subjectivity, for social intercourse. The exemplary difference between Augustine and Blake, then, would be that while Blake recognizes the use value of transcendental signifiers, he refuses to give them the ontological priority or perpetually fixed significance that Augustine does.

The opening plates of *Jerusalem* challenge the traditional exegetical reliance upon (an illegitimate) interpretive authority and revalue the inherent instability of tropological play which that tradition seeks to repress. Christian exegetes assert that instruction in their hermeneutical method provides for their audience an escape from the misery, fear, and oppression caused by its ignorance of the Divine Will. The Blakean revision demonstrates that this instruction and this metaphysics produce the *subjects* who participate in constructing precisely those conditions of suffering that the traditional Christian instruction claims to alleviate. The critical moment of vision for the Blakean reader comes when he or she realizes that the text encourages *and* subverts all recourse to transcendental signifiers or external vantage points as guarantees of significance. Consequently, I will be paying particularly close attention to the function of such signifiers in the opening plates.

> Of the Sleep of Ulro! and of the passage through
> Eternal Death! and of the awaking to Eternal Life .
>
> This theme calls me in sleep night after night & ev'ry morn
> Awakes me at sun-rise, then I see the Saviour over me
> Spreading his beams of love, & dictating the words of this mild
>   song.

The Fall from Hermeneutics and the Rhetoric of Subjectivity 69

> Awake! awake O sleeper of the land of shadows, wake! expand!
> I am in you and you in me, mutual in love divine:
> Fibres of love from man to man thro Albions pleasant land.
> In all the dark Atlantic vale down from the hills of Surrey
> A black water accumulates, return Albion! return!
> Thy brethren call thee. and thy fathers, and thy sons,
> Thy nurses and thy mothers, thy sisters and thy daughters
> Weep at thy souls disease. and the Divine Vision is darkend;
> Thy Emanation that was wont to play before thy face.
> Beaming forth with her daughters into the Divine bosom.
>   [*Where*]!!
> Where hast thou hidden thy Emanation lovely Jerusalem
> From the vision and fruition of the Holy-one?
> I am not a God afar off, I am a brother and friend;
> Within your bosoms I reside, and you reside in me:
> Lo! we are One; forgiving all Evil; Not seeking recompense !
> Ye are my members O ye sleepers of Beulah. land of shades!
>
> But the perturbed Man away turns down the valleys dark;
> [*Saying. We are not One: we are Many, thou most simulative*]
> Phantom of the over heated brain! shadow of immortality!
> Seeking to keep my soul a victim to thy Love! which binds
> Man the enemy of man into deceitful friendships:
> Jerusalem is not! her daughters are indefinite:
> By demonstration. man alone can live, and not by faith.
> My mountains are my own. and I will keep them to myself:
> The Malvern and the Cheviot. the Wolds Plinlimmon & Snowdon
> Are mine. here will I build my Laws of Moral Virtue,:
> Humanity shall be no more: but war & princedom & victory!
>
> So spoke Albion in jealous fears. hiding his Emanation
> Upon the Thames and Medway. rivers of Beulah: dissembling
> His jealousy before the throne divine, darkening. cold:
>
>   (Plate 4)

In the standard critical response to this plate, the passages of the third stanza, lines 6 through 21, are considered to be the voice of the Christian "Saviour" or Christ, while the passages of the fourth stanza, lines 24 through 32, are read as Albion's voice. Certainly the spatial divisions of these passages on the plate as well as the values Christianity gives to the concepts of love, forgiveness, and brotherhood encourage these identifications. Yet even within the first two lines disruptions in signification occur that multiply uncertainties throughout the plate.

"Of the Sleep of Ulro!" Who is speaking these lines? And what or who is Ulro?[3] The opening line seems to tell the reader not to worry about his or her lack of knowledge. Like *Paradise Lost*, the poem might be announcing its argument: if it is "about" the Sleep of Ulro, what follows, it could be assumed, will provide answers to these questions. A reader first encountering this line could easily think that Ulro is a character in the poem, perhaps even a main character, insofar as the name appears in the first line as the primary topic of the epic argument. Perhaps this character, the reader could justifiably reason, sleeps in a noteworthy way, or perhaps something noteworthy happens during its sleep. The second part of the line seems to reinforce the notion that Ulro is a character: "and of the passage through" implies that someone is doing the passing. That might be Ulro, although some other character (or the reader, or many other characters) might be passing through somewhere while Ulro is sleeping. Maybe Ulro is passing through its own sleep; yet again, maybe the sleep and the passage are two distinct actions.

However, "Of the Sleep of Ulro!" might be a declaration of participation rather than a description of the poem's argument. Something (what it may be remains unspecified) is possessed by the Sleep of Ulro, or perhaps the poem is proclaiming the fact of its belonging to the Sleep of Ulro. Or further, the poem might not be "about" the Sleep of Ulro but rather a reproduction or enactment of it. Difficulties are generated not only by these uncertainties—by the lack of identification of the space being traversed and of the one taking the journey—but also by the phrase's unclear syntactical relationship to the following line, "Eternal Death! and of the awaking to Eternal Life ." Does "passage through" refer to a journey through "Eternal Death"? If so, how can it be eternal? On the other hand, "Eternal Death!" may be a comment on the preceding line, a possibility which suggests that the conclusion of the first line might be read graphically as "the passage through [nowhere]."

This first line has a peculiar status, then. There is no clear identi-

---

3. It should be obvious by now that I regard virtually all of the commentary on Blake's work as exercises in fixing a fundamentally indeterminate text. I do not interpret the signifiers of Blake's text by reference to any of the scholarship that tries to create a symbol key or assumes the stability of the meaning of these signifiers across texts or even within them.

fication of an epic voice, because at least one plausible reading subverts the convention of an opening epic argument. There is no clear identification of the entity that the prepositional phrase "Of . . ." modifies in either of the parts of the line, nor is it possible to determine the signification of "of." There is no clear identification of the nature of Ulro. There is no clear identification of the space being passed through, nor of the agent conducting the passage. Modifiers with nothing to modify; possessives belonging to no one; spaces located nowhere; signifiers that shift location and reference—whatever, whoever, and wherever the first line signifies, it is an uncomfortable place for the reader to linger.

Indeterminate agency and a movement from nowhere to nowhere by no one in particular—these might be features of an Eternal Death, a perpetual "passing through" without getting anywhere, a kind of Limbo. Thus, the second line might serve to relieve the reader's discomfort not only by supplying a narrative telos for the passage (something or someone gets to Eternal Life, although the specification of the agent remains obscure) but also by naming and objectifying the reader's experience. From this point of view, "and of the awaking to Eternal Life ." functions as thematic content, holding out a hope for future clarification (as part of the argument of the poem) *and* as metacommentary, self-reflexively remarking upon a condition of (at least partial) enlightenment as the reader "passes" from textual indeterminacy to determinacy. The relatively unfamiliar idea of an Eternal Death that can be passed through (at some cost to its status as an eternal state) is countered here by reference to the overly familiar Christian notion of an Eternal Life. Once the reader reaches this place of familiarity and determinacy, he or she likely will assign agency, narrativity, and genre in such a way as to reproduce it.

So, despite the initial disturbance to the reader's equanimity, by the end of the second line the poem seems to be asserting that it is a (somewhat didactic) Christian epic, a *Pilgrim's Progress* perhaps, even if the pilgrim remains unseen. The unspecified agency and the indeterminate location of the first line can be accommodated to the Miltonic tradition: this is the Christian Muse speaking, the Divinity who is ineffable and ubiquitous. If it seems odd that the Eternal Life—that ultimate condition of revelation and grace in Christian doctrine—is not welcomed with the extra verve of an exclamation point, if some questions remain about what "Ulro" means, even if the whole project seems a little hackneyed, all this can be attributed to the reader's need for instruction—the most common Augustinian topos—which the poem, in the fullness of time, will supply.

A traditional Christian understanding of this plate—which would emphasize the division of the passages into a dialogue between a Christian Saviour and a fallen Albion—would take the position that the Saviour is calling Albion's attention to his "souls disease," that is, to his ignorance of his true relationship to this Divinity who promises immortality through identification with itself. Albion is misguided, unnecessarily alienated, and in mortal danger, so this reading goes, because he does not realize that his true identity is to be found in a transcendent vision of communitarian selflessness. On this understanding, the Saviour would be seen as offering a charitable reading of all the texts of the land of shades, while Albion somehow misunderstands the Saviour's love, seeing it as a trap rather than as redemption. Albion's attack on love ("Seeking to keep my soul a victim to thy Love! which binds / Man the enemy of man into deceitful friendships:") would indicate, from an Augustinian viewpoint, that Albion does not know how to interpret the Scriptures charitably to discover God's message of love.

However, a series of interpretive dilemmas that makes this reading increasingly problematic confronts the reader who insists on maintaining that the signifiers "Eternal," "Saviour," "Divine," or "Holy-one" refer to the absolute values they have within a Christian discourse. As I noted in an earlier section, the poem undermines the authority of its ostensible epic voice. Furthermore, syntactical considerations make it impossible to determine whether the passage beginning "Awake! awake O sleeper of the land of shadows, wake! expand!" is a recitation of the "words of this mild song" that the Saviour is "dictating," whether the referent of "sleeper" is the "me" of the preceding lines or "Albion" of the subsequent lines, or even whether all of the statements of this passage are made by the same voice. The lines spoken by the poem's narrator are juxtaposed with those of a voice exhorting the sleeper to awake; these lines refer to Albion in the third person ("Albions pleasant land"), producing ambiguity about the identity of the sleeper. This confusion is heightened when the subsequent lines shift from third person to a direct address to Albion as an entity separate from the narrator, the voice of the "Saviour," and the exhorting voice, a situation that contradicts this speaker's claims that it and Albion are "One." This confusion is thematized in these passages' apparent conflict over who has the authority to define Albion's identity (not to mention Jerusalem's and her daughters'), a confusion that continues to shape the rhetoric and syntax of the plate. For example, the transitional sentence between the two final passages—"But the perturbed Man away turns down the valleys dark;"—suggests that both the voice presented as the Saviour and the voice presented as Albion are comprehended by "Man," as would be the case in the parable of the sheep and the goats; furthermore, "perturbed" means "crowded," suggesting that whoever the "Man" is, he has a multiple identity.

Without ultimately valorizing Albion's views, which are so clearly marked with a negative valence ("jealous fears," "dissembling," "darkening"), it is possible to see that his observations have force. Why should Albion give up his individual identity to become "merged" with another who claims the status of a divinity yet who itself suggests that it may not be a God at all ("I am not a God afar off.")? Why should Albion trust a being whose knowledge is far from the omniscience traditionally claimed as the source of divine authority? Such submission could be a kind of "Eternal Death." "Where hast thou hidden thy Emanation lovely Jerusalem / From the vision and fruition of the Holy-one?" not only disarticulates the identity of this voice from that of the "Holy-one," but also indicates that this voice has no special knowledge of Albion, despite its claim to be part of him. And how is it possible for the "Divine Vision" to be "darkend" or occluded by the actions of a "Man"? If one of these voices is claiming a special status for itself as God that it in fact does not have, then Albion's refusal of its terms ceases to seem like the classic behavior of the willfully blind sinner and begins to take on the qualities of a legitimate self-defense.

An interpretation that regards Albion's contentions as justifiable—an interpretation that emphasizes the dangers of granting a single identity and authority to all of the propositions made in this section of the plate—would remark on the contradictory nature of those propositions. How can "Albions pleasant land" be both a place of mutuality, where fibres of love connect everyone, *and* a place of accumulating black water, where Albion is isolated, unless the two descriptions are equivalent, which makes "fibres of love" acquire a negative valence (precisely Albion's point about binding man to man in "deceitful friendships")? Or unless the descriptions issue from two different vantage points, which destroys the unity of the identity of the source of these lines, a consequence antithetical to the Christian interpretation? Or perhaps one situation follows the other temporally or causally, which suggests that the "fibres of love" cause the black water to accumulate (as the convergence of the fibres graphically displayed at the bottom half of the plate into the black edges and night sky might suggest)? Or it may be that there is no explanation for the shift in the subsequent lines, neither of which is compatible with a Christian reading.

If a second reading of Albion's assertion of his self-possession counteracts the traditional Christian reading which would stage a conflict between a unified Christian divine voice and an alienated fallen voice, it does so by destabilizing the unity and transcendence of the divinity. And even though at least one of the multiple voices in these passages claims that multiplicity and secularization as a positive value—a value compatible with a traditional vantage point that regards Christians as the members of Christ's body—the convolved identity of "I am in you and you in me" also recasts Albion's possessiveness as his multiplicity ("Albions pleasant land," "thy souls disease"), thereby giving Albion the same status as the voice of Christian salvation and once again disrupting the special authority of that voice. If Albion and the voice of reciprocal identity are truly inseparable, then both err in regarding Albion as a separate being, not only capable of separating himself from the voice, his relatives, and his friends, but also intent on separating his Emanation from "the Holy-one." In other words, the voice or voices calling to Albion in these lines reinscribe a separation it or they deny is either desirable or possible. It is worth noting in this context that the Greek inscription at the top of the plate (*Monos o Iesous*), translated by Bloom as "Jesus only," means "Solitary Jesus," suggesting a reading of this plate that insists on Albion's solitude as a sign of his identity and his distance from Jesus.

It is impossible in the first lines of the passage to disentangle

The Fall from Hermeneutics and the Rhetoric of Subjectivity   75

identity from positions of relationship, making it difficult to categorize what is being identified: are these beings, subjects, conditions of existence? These initial lines describe an ontological situation in which no subject position has priority or has an identity that can be defined except in relation to other subject positions. By the end of the passage, however, the claims of multiplicity and mutuality are transfigured, first into an assertion of a unity that collapses one identity into another, and second into an expression of the domination of that identity over another, a domination figured as appropriation: "I am in you and you in me, mutual in love divine:" does not indicate the same relationship as "Lo! we are One . . . / Ye are my members." In fact, these are quite different relationships. Not only do the lines between them persistently emphasize separation, ignorance, guilt, and lack of understanding, so that the return to claims of reciprocal identification in "Within your bosoms I reside, and you reside in me;" sound hollow, but also this formulation marks a subtle change from an emphasis on an intermingled identity ("I am in you and you in me, mutual") to separable identities ("Within your bosoms I reside"). Furthermore, in the next line the idea of intermingled identification gives way to a figure in which one side of the identification takes precedence: "Ye are my members" assigns priority to its own identity and position. The passage moves from one configuration to another—from "I am in you and you in me, mutual in love divine:" to "Within your bosoms I reside, and you reside in me;" "Lo! we are One;" and "Ye are my members"—as though reacting to the initial proposition of mutual, intermingled, relational identity by insisting, with increasing force, on hierarchy, opposition, fixity, alienation, and possessiveness.

This movement culminates in "Albions" subsequent lines, where we find assertions almost completely governed by the insistence on these values: "Are mine. here will I build my Laws of Moral Virtue,! / Humanity shall be no more: but war & princedom and victory!" embodies the links among hierarchy, alienation, domination, and a strategy for dealing with indeterminacy by legislating it out of existence. At the same time, however, this section of the plate also has a multivocal quality: although some of these propositions seem antithetical to the doctrine of mutuality advanced by some of the voices of the preceding passages, others support it, as in the lines "Jerusalem is not! her daughters are indefinite: / By demonstration. man alone can live, and not by faith." These lines can be read as an affirmation of reciprocal identity, a refusal of the preceding passage's unfounded separation of Albion from Emanation and Emanation from Holy-one. To say that "Jerusalem is not!" might be to say that Jerusalem does not exist autonomously; to say that "her daughters are indefinite" might be to say that the true ontological status of all of the beings indicated by the entire plate is convolved, not defined or delimited—as "demonstrated" by the passages themselves. Finally, to say "man alone can live, and not by faith" might be to say that when man lives without faith, man lives a solitary life—again, an assertion demonstrably true from a Christian vantage point. Thus, this vaunting passage does not emerge as misguided opposition to a redemptive viewpoint but rather continues and consolidates the gestures and strategies of what precedes it.

The "Saviour"'s passage sets out two possible responses to its initial conditions of indeterminate, multiple identity: either the identities are collapsed into "One," which negates the identities comprehended within the multiple identifications of the first lines, or the identities are separated and placed in conflict. It is important to note that either response inscribes a hierarchical organization, which implies relations of domination and submission. It ought to come as no surprise, then, to find that the history of Blake criticism wearisomely repeats these same gestures and strategies, remarking time and time again on the radical differences between the "Saviour" and "Albion," between self-centeredness and selflessness, or between the forms of hierarchy, negation, and possessiveness present in the "Saviour"'s speech and those forms in "Albions," despite the plate's presentation of their fundamental similarities.[4]

The plate enacts a struggle for authority; the problem of the provenance and geography of the opening lines of the poem emerges as the topic of the next lines, in which the confusion about the "origin"

---

4. Numerous examples of this critical history can be found, but one of the most recent is paradigmatic: Peter Otto's discussion of this plate, while providing an intelligent description of "Albion's" fallen point of view, ignores all the problematic features of the plate and simply redefines each signifier in terms of an allegory of Christian doctrine (*Constructive Vision and Visionary Deconstruction*, 14–15).

of the poem appears. This confusion apparently calls for a stabilizing response: hence the insistence in the face of unclear agency and inspecific power relations on an agent of salvation, a "Saviour" who seems to fulfill the traditional function of the Christian Messiah ("Spreading his beams of love") but whose next action ("dictating the words of this mild song") contradicts the previous lines, mischaracterizes the nature of the poem we are reading, and establishes a disturbing echo of "Albions" charge against his interlocutor(s) and "Albions" own desires for mastery. This recourse to a stabilizing transcendent signifier fails conspicuously, generating increasingly frequent ambiguities about the appropriate claims of authority in the dialogue section of the plate, a section which stages the very problem this transcendental signifier is supposed to resolve. Nothing in the plate provides a context within which the legitimacy of one or another voice can be adjudicated; any attempt to use the Christian doctrine of identification in Christ as such a context results in the reflexive criticism that the "Christian" position of the Saviour does not conform to the doctrine.

Throughout the plate, the confusions of identity provoke repeated attempts to individuate what may be multiple: the transcendental signifiers serve the purpose of stabilizing an unstable opposition by promoting the illusion that a context within which that opposition finds its ground exists prior to the linguistic universe of the text. The application of particular criteria that "prove" authority or certainty, such as Augustine's test for "charitableness"—and the enactment of strategies of containment, limitation, and exclusion that create the illusion of legitimate authority in the scene of reading/interpretation—expose the presence of ideological structures available to the reader at any given historical moment. Because the point of mediation of all ideologies is the individual mind, which is constituted in the dialogical arena of ideologies bidding for hegemony (that is, for the authority to constitute "the real"), Blake's text has the potential for revealing both public and private ideological structures. Nonetheless, it would be a mistake to assume that Blake's exposure of the tropological strategies by which authority disguises the source of its ideological power leads automatically to some sort of liberatory or redemptive moment. In his shift from hermeneutics to rhetoric, a shift which entails the unmasking of the illegitimate presumption of an "ultimate" authority, Blake not only exposes these strategies as necessary for the production of *any* textual authority but also traces the processes by which subjectivities are constituted by hegemonic discursive practices. In the following sections, we will analyze whether there is a difference, finally, between Blake's strategies for disseminating authority and the hegemonic strategies that displace and disguise the representations of their origins—in other words, whether the Blakean text provides any resistance to oppression that does not (like Los's struggles with Hand) ultimately reproduce the forms of error it strives against.

Epistemological Crisis and the Phenomenalistic Subject

The links between strategies for producing "natural" language, denotative reference, interpretive authority, and stable identities that Blake explores in the opening and closing plates of *Jerusalem* depend at some level on the question of whether or not there is a fundamental resemblance between mind and world. It is not surprising to find this issue prominently featured in Blake's work. The "de-signing" of authority traced by political and literary thinkers of the seventeenth and eighteenth centuries effected discursive transformations within and across disciplinary boundaries. A notable—and crucial for contemporary philosophy—consequence of these transformations is the development of philosophies of mind that linked political, economic, psychological, linguistic, and biological descriptions of human subjectivity. One of the most important examples of this new discursive linking, and one of the most forceful depictions of the consequences of the displacement of authority, for eighteenth-century thinkers is Hobbes's description of the "state of war" in *Leviathan*; Hobbes's work comprises a significant response to the radical destabilization of authority that attended England's Civil

War. His characterization of atomistic individuals compelled by their passions to compete with one another for possessions and prestige represents the extreme effects of a loss of ultimate authority; each individual, left to its own devices, is not even an authority over itself but a victim of internal forces and appetites, which may be incommensurable and over which it has no control. From Hobbes and Locke to Hume and Hartley, the urgency for rethinking the grounds for legitimating authority appears in theories of subjectivity that, from a contemporary point of view, both characterize and deconstruct Enlightenment humanism.

In the late eighteenth century, anxieties about the profoundly ungrounded nature of authority frequently took the form of an assertion that mind and nature fundamentally resembled one another, or as Coleridge puts it in the *Biographia Literaria*, "the theory of natural philosophy would then be completed, when all nature was demonstrated to be identical in essence with that, which in its highest known power exists in man as intelligence and self-consciousness."[5] These anxieties were sufficiently intense to generate several philosophical systems designed to defend against the more radical implications of a skeptical empiricism that insisted on the possibility that there was no ontological guarantee for a compatibility between subject and object. The philosophical strategies employed to fend off this possibility were much discussed well into the nineteenth century in the intellectual organs on both sides of the channel. Joseph Johnson's *The Analytical Review* published numerous articles devoted to reviewing the philosophical commentaries exploring this issue. In January 1797, Johnson published a substantial review of F. A. Nitsch's *A gen-*

---

5. *Biographia Literaria*, chapter 22, in *Selected Poetry and Prose*, ed. Donald A. Stauffer, 243. Coleridge's own attempt to reconcile the "essences" of subject and object appears in this chapter, and it is clear that Coleridge is responding to Humean arguments that it is not possible to know with certainty whether the material world or even mind actually exists. Coleridge's "demonstration" depends upon two arguments: first, that there are no grounds for assuming that things exist without us—"the philosopher therefore compels himself to treat this faith as nothing more than a prejudice"; second, that there are no grounds for certainty that subjects exist—the idea of the existence of mind "is groundless indeed." Finally, Coleridge effects the *identification* of nature and mind on the grounds of their groundlessness and asserts that they must be in essence the same: "it [nature] is not only coherent but identical, and one and the same thing with our own immediate self-consciousness" (245).

eral and introductory View of Professor Kant's Principles . . . submitted to the Consideration of the Learned (Downes, 1796), a work that not only translated and summarized Kant but also provided an overview of the predominant philosophical positions that attempted to reconcile subject and object.[6]

The review of Nitsch's book makes it clear that the reviewer expected the audience to be familiar with these positions. Following Nitsch, the reviewer briefly outlines the debates among them. The materialist position, the reviewer claims, argues that matter exists essentially as extension and that our minds must also in essence be material objects, capable of a knowledge of matter by virtue of a "mechanical faculty of *organization*" that merely sorts the sensations that experience impresses upon the material substance of the mind. The rationalists (idealists) observe that extension need not be granted priority as an essential characteristic of real objects; they deny "existence of the external world, and made the power of knowledge consist in reason alone." The spiritualists, "from their pretended knowledge of spirits and immaterial objects, whose essential property they have discovered to be simplicity, assert a power of knowing spirits and immaterial objects, as well as material, and make this power to be a compound of the faculties of sense, understanding, and reason." In each case, the reviewer asserts, these sects confuse the ques-

6. The earliest translation of Kant appeared in English in 1796, his "Project for a perpetual peace." An exposition of Kant's critique, entitled "The principles of critical philosophy selected from the works of Emmanuel Kant" by James Sigismund Beck, was published by Blake's friend, publisher, and employer, Joseph Johnson. Both Blake's friendship with Johnson and his work for the publisher make it plausible that he was aware of Kant's enterprise. The review of Nitsch's translation and summary of Kant discussed here, entitled "Nitsch's *Introductory View of Kant's Principles*," begins: "The philosophy of Mr. Kant, which, in this country, is but partially known, has on the continent been much studied, and by the philosophers of Germany, as we have been informed, pretty generally adopted. The celebrity, which it's author has there acquired, as a moralist and metaphysician, is unquestionably very great, and whatever judgment may be pronounced respecting his principles as true or false, we have no hesitation in admitting that the reputation, which his elaborate and profound speculations have procured to him, is the just reward, and indeed the necessary concomitant of genius and patient industry united" (11).

I will be referring to the review of Nitsch's summary in the following discussion, on the grounds that this is the most likely source of Blake's knowledge of Kant. The next quotations are from this review, 14.

tion of the source of the power of knowledge with the question of the essence of things, assuming improperly that their "arbitrary notions of the essential properties of the things around them" enable them to "derive" the nature of the power of knowledge. Even the skeptics, according to this review, who confess that they do not know the nature of things, assume a resemblance between mind, thing, and word when they assert that they cannot know the truth about the nature of mind as a consequence of their ignorance of things.

Nitsch asserts that Kant takes a different view, rejecting the petitio principii that informs these arguments, by asserting that there is no necessary resemblance between mind and world.[7] Kant objects that these thinkers have derived their ideas of mind from their ideas of nature rather than, as he deemed proper, the other way around. Kant postulates an alternative relationship between mind and world, concluding that the mind "experiences" the "world" only as a series of intuitions that bear no necessary resemblance to any ontologically prior external actuality. Although this position seems to lead directly to solipsism, Kant nevertheless affirms it, in order to assert the higher value of freedom: he claims that such a mind is cut free from the constraints of externalities and placed in a position of ultimate liberty and creativity. As Nitsch summarizes him, Kant argues:

> But time, as well as space, are not properties of things; they are only the general forms under which man is allowed to view himself and the world. . . . It follows, therefore, *that man is not in time and space*, although the forms of his intuitive ideas are time and space. *If man exist not in time and space, he is not influenced by the laws of time and space, among which those of cause and effect hold a distinguished rank*; it is, therefore, no contradiction to conceive, that, in such an order of things, man may be free.[8]

---

7. Nitsch claims that for Kant, "scepticism" entailed the assertion that the external world did not exist, when Nitsch is arguing that Kant is no skeptic. However, in his first characterization, he acknowledges that the skeptical position simply means that we do not know "the true and essential properties of things" ("Nitsch's *Introductory View*, 14). Clearly, Kant is not a skeptic insofar as he constructs a transcendental subjectivity to block the implications of the skeptical position he resorts to at crucial moments. In any event, the skeptical position does not ever get a full expression in eighteenth-century philosophy, but, as with the case of Hume, for example, not all skeptics resorted to the necessity of the resemblance between mind and world.

8. "Nitsch's *Introductory View*," 19.

In order to defend against the imputation of solipsism—Kant's major objection to the Humean radical skepticism his own thought otherwise reproduces—Kant asserts that "an idea of practical reason," which itself exists out of time and space, governs the will of man. Kant uses that "idea" as a springboard to his constructions of universal "moral law" and a transcendental subjectivity, constructions that effectively forestall the slide into solipsism insofar as they postulate universal principles of reason that conform to the teleological "ends" of man.[9]

Throughout *Jerusalem*, Blake keeps this issue before the reader. Blake does not stage the problem simply as a conflict between a "subjective" and an "objective" position: in Blake's work, it is not a question of mind recognizing the prior claims of reality, but rather a question of facing the difficulties of the radical skeptical position. *Jerusalem* dramatizes the competing claims of subjective accounts, as in Plate 4, among which there are no external standards for adjudicating truth but instead only contested claims for authority based on various ungrounded metaphysical presuppositions, including the presupposition of the autonomous existence of external reality. In fact, as I will show in the penultimate section, it is precisely the assumption of the existence of an objective reality—independent of the constructions of mind—that transforms the potentially liberatory phenomenalistic subject into the dominating possessive Selfhood and establishes the conditions for oppression.

The Blakean text affirms the value of the Kantian insight that mind resembles world because mind constitutes world, but Blake—as he does in his transformation of Augustinian precepts—refuses the Kantian defense against solipsism, the turn to transcendent sub-

9. I want to note that in the ensuing discussion when I refer to a critique of metaphysics I am referring to a critique of all a priori assumptions, including the assumption that external reality and mind bear any necessary resemblance. When Kant uses the term *metaphysics*, he refers first to the systematic presentation of nonempirical philosophy. The Kantian project begins with a Humean epistemological critique, and its transcendentalism emerges from its suspension of any reliance upon assumptions about empirical reality. Kant's assumptions about the universalistic nature of pure reason, however, constitute a metaphysical assumption that he does not critique. It ought to be clear, then, that when I refer to an antimetaphysical position, I am arguing that Kant criticizes a certain set of metaphysical assumptions in order to reinstate metaphysics both explicitly and implicitly at another level.

Epistemological Crisis and the Phenomenalistic Subject 83

jectivity and universal moral laws. The Kantian echoes in the boast "here will I build my Laws of Moral Virtue" (Plate 4) indicate one link between the phenomenalistic subject's tendency to solipsism ("Phantom of the over heated brain!") and the erection of some "transcendental" guarantee of the "validity" of its limited viewpoint The move to transcendental subjectivity and universal moral laws, the Blakean texts show, is a *manifestation* of the tendency of the phenomenalistic subject to deny its inadequacies, its spatiotemporal limitations: the Kantian assertion that reason has a divine provenance and mission reflects the need on the part of that limited subjectivity to believe that the limits of subjective knowledge demarcate the actual boundaries of what can be known, of what there *is* to be known.

Jerusalem presents an alternative understanding of subjectivity, one that maintains the epistemological priority of the subject and provides a defense against solipsism without illicitly importing metaphysical guarantees. The Blakean text argues for the discursive formation of mind as well as the discursive formation of what counts as reality for mind. On this view (shared by several skeptical empiricists, Hume and James Mill among them), lack of access to an external reality that could guarantee the validity of knowledge does not relegate all knowledge to the status of idiosyncratic fantasizing on the part of self-centered solipsists. By insisting on the discursive constitution of subjectivity, Blake could still maintain the time- and space-altering capabilities of human beings without recapitulating the conditions of solipsism. In the next two sections, I discuss the two possibilities (and Blake's response to them) that emerged historically for an understanding of a transformative subjectivity on grounds that grant primacy to the notion that semiotic or ideological constructions produce the only "reality" important to subjects. These two possibilities are the "typological subject" and the "subject of discourse": the claims for a need to transform subjects as well as the arguments for particular conditions and techniques of transformation that are made on behalf of these two types of subjects depend on a description of a phenomenalistic subject. This description derives ultimately from the work of the radical empiricists and reappears in phenomenological thinking from Kant to Husserl. This phenomenalistic subject is the focus of Blake's own analytic, and it is central to my discussion of the extent to which Blake's views on the constitution of subjectivity represent a utopian or emancipatory potential.

Many commentators have noted the presence of an apparent paradox in Blake's work, a paradox that reiterates the Kantian solution to the skeptical problem in a different form. When Blake articulates the primacy of individual perceptions, he apparently locates the individual mind both as a source of problems—solipsism, Hobbesian competition—and as the vehicle for redemption, ostensibly by providing humankind with the means for creating an identification in "One Man." Scholarship has typically reinscribed the fundamental philosophical arguments this tension generates. Between the multeity of individual perceptions and identities and a hoped-for unity of existence lies philosophical ground traditionally traversed by empiricism or idealism. Either the world can be abstracted to a set of universals from particular phenomena (thereby permitting the comprehension of essences as a function of the empirical world) or everyone has the same fundamental perceptual "apparatus" (which makes the world appear unified as a function of consciousness). Because Blake's texts so frequently reiterate a contempt for "abstraction," the empiricist model is seldom selected as a solution to the paradox.

But the idealist model creates its own problems, both internally and with respect to Blake's texts. Leopold Damrosch's excursus on this problem, *Symbol and Truth in Blake's Myth*, can stand as one of the most thoughtful discussions of the paradox *and* as an example of the difficulties the idealist position creates for Blake critics. Damrosch concludes that Blake must ultimately propose a universal or transcendental consciousness in order to bridge the gap between individual solipsistic perception and the alleged unity of humanity. Damrosch argues that Blake wishes to abolish the distinction between subject and object because "you can only remain *yourself* by not being attached to your self."[10] According to Damrosch, individual identity is the problem, solipsism the danger, and transcendental consciousness the solution.

However, Damrosch's view that by collapsing subject and object we can be "at one with a universal order in which we possess every-

---

10. *Symbol and Truth*, 147.

thing that we desire, and desire nothing that we cannot possess" misses the point of Blake's depictions of the construction of subjectivity.[11] Although it is true that Blake's portrayals of individual subjectivity frequently emphasize the negative qualities associated with the phenomenalistic self, for example as expressed in Plate 4, the various descriptions of subjectivity are by no means consistent across Blake's corpus nor are they insusceptible of alternative interpretation, as the reading I offered in the preceding section shows. The example of "annihilation" of the possessive selfhood is particularly important: Damrosch quotes Milton's speech to his Spectre to support his contention that Blake's ultimate response to the problems posed by individualism is the *subversion* of individual identity or the *submersion* of individual identity in that of a transcendent being. But Milton's voice is not the authoritative voice in the poem, nor does Blake reiterate this version of annihilation of the selfhood in *Jerusalem*. At the conclusion of the poem, individual identity is maintained even in "Eternity," and individual perception continues to vary, even after the "apocalypse" of Albion's awakening into "Fourfold" existence.

Despite the importance of Damrosch's insight that the "status of the self" in Blake's work is difficult to discern, and despite the power of Damrosch's mind and the impressive scope of his book, his difficulty in conceptualizing the Blakean subject derives precisely *from* his method, not from Blake's practice. As intellectual history, Damrosch's book, like others of its genre, suffers from three misconceptions that virtually force his conclusion that Blake insists upon a transcendental subjectivity. First, Damrosch makes no distinction between statements in the poems, the letters, the commentaries, or the early or late works; this means that the corpus itself comes to stand in for Blake's consciousness. Second, he treats all of the statements in Blake's corpus as though they represented Blake's own position; his lack of attention to the context in which these statements are uttered leads him to posit a kind of "omnisubjectivity" (to use his own word for what he claims Blake proposes). Damrosch's

---

11. It is a sign of the complexity of Blake's descriptions that Northrop Frye claims that Blake's *hell* is where "the distinction of subject and object is lost" (*Fearful Symmetry*, 48), precisely Damrosch's portrayal of Blake's *heaven* (*Symbol and Truth*, 132).

complaint that "for all his praise of particulars, Blake never shows much interest in human uniqueness" in fact describes Damrosch's own treatment of Blake's texts: the particularity, the rhetorical specificity of statements uttered in the poems, is sacrificed to the assumption that the corpus itself must be unified.[12] Third, this fallacy of a unified and invariant Blakean position extends to the method of analogizing from particular propositions found in Blake to particular propositions found in other thinkers, as though analogies could serve as analytical tools, or as though all of intellectual history, from the Greeks through the twentieth century, participates in the same discursive arena, using constant terms and taking up universal problems. Again, Damrosch's description of the Blakean self serves as a description of his own covert assumptions: Blake "insists that the self [read "intellectual history"] is atemporal, and will admit no accumulated weight of experience."[13]

An interesting nexus of assumptions haunts Damrosch's text. He regards the various lexemes he quotes from throughout Blake's corpus as given, that is, as individual assertions belonging to a unified philosophical position and as expressions of Blake's psychological state. Hence, Blake's texts exist for Damrosch as a unified repository of propositions that are not to be *read* in the strong sense but rather are to be evaluated as true or false by reference to other theoretical systems (such as Freud's or Cusanus's or Boehme's) with which Blake may or may not have been familiar. So, for example, statements such as "I do not deny that analogues to Blake's position may be found in Boehme and elsewhere; I deny that they make sense" indicate Damrosch's interest in assuming the unity of Blake's thought as available in a propositional form as well as his belief that his standard of what "makes sense" somehow applies ahistorically and acontextually for the duration of Western intellectual history.[14] The *textuality* of Blake's work is ignored, as are the sophistications of its rhetorical strategies. It is no surprise, then, to find Damrosch referring to modern phenomenology, because his treatment of the corpus-as-consciousness accords precisely with the principles of practition-

12. *Symbol and Truth*, 151.
13. Ibid., 161.
14. Ibid., 238.

ers of literary phenomenology, most notably Georges Poulet.[15] One unacknowledged consequence of these assumptions is that Damrosch reproduces as theoretical premise the conditions linking the production of a phenomenalistically centralized subject as the origin and guarantor of a determinate meaning with a purely referential or positivistic concept of signification.

Jerusalem also demonstrates the connections among a centralized subject, invoked as the origin and guarantor of a determinate meaning, referentiality, and conditions of social oppression. Contrary to Damrosch's claims, Blake maintains the phenomenalistic self as the source of the potential for liberatory practice, rather than simply targeting it for "annihilation." In order to understand Blake's conception of the construction of subjectivity—its dangers and possibilities—it is crucial to regard the later poems, as W. J. T. Mitchell once remarked, as "gymnasiums for the mind," not as philosophical documents or systems of propositional statements. The utterances in these texts function rhetorically rather than declaratively. Attending to the rhetorical contexts within which these utterances appear makes clear that Blake consistently refuses the universalistic or transcendental solution that Damrosch himself occults as his analytic premise. In the Blakean text, the problem with the possessive Selfhood is that it tyrannizes over a world that it conceives solely in terms of its properties and its ability to be possessed—a world, in other words, susceptible to abstraction and to governance by "One Law," to *universalization*.

One way to understand the position of this subject is to view it as standing at the center of a phenomenalistically produced horizon, a position that emphasizes relationships of domination. The absolute

---

15. Paul De Man's discussion of Poulet's assumptions about the body of an author's writings corresponding to the unity of authorial consciousness is relevant here (see *Blindness and Insight: Essays in the Rhetoric of Contemporary Criticism*). It is entirely consistent with Damrosch's analogistic practices that he quotes Augustine on the value of similitude: "As didactic writers from Augustine to Bunyan reiterate, we learn the most from 'similitudes' that demand mental efforts; and a quite similar case could be made in terms of a modern phenomenology of reading." But Damrosch does not include the remainder of the Augustine quotation from *On Christian Doctrine*, which contains Augustine's own criticism of "similitude"—that it articulates difference as well as identity—a criticism that Damrosch's method must lead him to repress.

demarcation between subject and object that this selfhood produces, however, is merely a consequence of an illusion, a kind of optico-theoretical illusion. The selfhood that insists on its own centrality—*not* as a function of its phenomenalistic position but rather as a *right*—has repressed the extent to which its relationship to the world is a function of its perceptual limitations. What the selfhood takes to be a central position—a position of ultimate mastery—in fact amounts to an enslavement in a severely circumscribed universe where the ego seems central. In terms of perception, the central subject takes a perceptually inadequate stance and treats it as ultimate, complete, and authoritative. By the same token, however, these limitations are absolutely necessary for perception to take place at all.

Several commentators have noted that Blake's insistence upon individual perception hints at a phenomenological bias, although they agree that phenomenology is inadequate as a theoretical framework for understanding Blake's version of the subject. Hazard Adams remarks on Blake's affinities and departures from certain phenomenological principles: language in the service of reason has a tendency to "tyrannize over our imagination and dehumanize our experience, fictionalize it in the old Lockean way. . . . With the spirit of this phenomenological return to concrete actuality Blake would be in sympathy." Yet the unmediated experience of phenomena, Adams explains, as postulated by the phenomenologists, does not provide the materials for Blake's construction of "eternal forms": these must be realized through the medium of language. Although twentieth-century phenomenology, in its derivation from Kant, has its own transcendental project—the Husserlian account of the mediation of perception, the phenomenalistic position of the perceiving subject, and the relational forms between subject and object that arise from that position—it is useful to outline the phenomenological analysis as a way of gaining access to Blake's views on the limits and potentialities of the phenomenalistic self.[16]

Husserl begins with the "simplest" acts of consciousness—acts of perception which, however, can never be immediate. It is possible, Husserl explains, to have a purely sensory experience, but such an experience has no content for consciousness. Every perceptual act

---

16. See Adams, "Blake and the Postmodern," 16–17.

Epistemological Crisis and the Phenomenalistic Subject 89

involving an object will occur by reference to (*in virtue of*, in Husserlian terminology) one or some combination of the aspects of the object: its color, size, shape, use, or relation to other objects will vary depending upon the stance (both spatiotemporal and motivational) toward the object. Husserl gives the name *noema* to the particular content of the object that consciousness grasps. The *noemata* of the object—which are not a priori as the Kantian categories of space and time are—permit it to be perceived in its particularity, as this object rather than another. As such, the *noemata* establish identity and difference. Consciousness consists in this process of differentiation, which can never come to an end because some aspect of the object is always hidden from consciousness due to the spatiotemporal or cognitive limitations of the subject. The indeterminacy of the object—the inability of the subject to grasp the object completely in one intentional act—becomes part of the experience of the object for the subject. Therefore, the field of consciousness is bounded by a ring of indeterminacy, the point at which consciousness is not perceiving objects as particularities, as intentionally meaningful, but only as objects in the abstract, as potentially meaningful.[17] This ring of indeterminacy Husserl calls the "horizon": "What is actually perceived and what is more or less clearly co-present and determinate (to some extent at least), is partly pervaded, partly girt about with a *dimly apprehended depth or fringe of indeterminate reality*. . . . Moreover, the zone of indeterminacy is infinite. The misty horizon that can never be completely outlined remains necessarily there."[18] The sense or meaning of the object for consciousness depends not only upon its *noema*, fixed by consciousness during the intentional act, but also upon the indeterminate nature of the object. The object can only be perceived as such when it is given a particular identity, which at the same time bestows a limit upon that identity, a place

---

17. It is important to note that I am not using the term *perception* in the sense of the simple registering of photons upon the retina, or electrical impulses upon the brain, but the active perception that consciousness recognizes as perception *of* something, what Husserl calls the "intentional act." The term "intentional" might be misleading, however, insofar as we normally associate intentionality with consciousness. For Husserl, the object participates in the intentional act and helps to produce consciousness. This undecidability of origin or intention parallels the undecidabilities of Plate 97, which I discuss below.

18. *Ideas: General Introduction to Pure Phenomenology*, 92.

where the object merges into everything else, a reservoir of potential identity/meaning.

This ring of indeterminacy, this "horizon," constantly draws the subject into intending new acts of consciousness in order to grasp the object completely, to fix its meaning once and for all. In the opening plate of *Jerusalem*, Albion's response to the voice's exhortation to become "One" with it would seem to be a logical response by a subjectivity for whom consciousness and identity depend upon absolute differentiation. By the same token, Albion's opening speech defensively represses knowledge of the limitations of its phenomenalistic position, a repression that in Husserlian terms would treat the "horizon" not as a reservoir of potentialities but as an absolute limit beyond which nothing else exists. The negation of the potential meanings beyond the grasp of the centralized subject corresponds to the negation of other relational forms between subject and object.

In this context, one value of Albion's opening speech inheres in its exposure of the production of this type of subjectivity: in his speech, Albion still is capable of remarking upon *his* construction of the world, his imposition of authority, his assertion of ownership. Albion acknowledges the violence to other subjects implicit in his decision: "Humanity shall be no more" because all subjects will be reduced to the status of objects. Furthermore, he indicates the means by which it is possible to establish the fiction that authority is not self-designed but derives from some unassailable source when he affirms that he will "build" his "Moral Law"; this "Moral Law" not only has the capability of masking his self-promotion but also "justifies" the illicit violence by which it is maintained. Thus, the emergence of the possessive Selfhood at this moment in the poem retains the traces of its own deconstruction. In Blake's terms, Albion's description of this extreme version of individual subjectivity represents the "limit of contraction" beyond which it is impossible for human beings to degenerate. The regenerative potential in this limit of contraction is the acknowledgment that the subject position has produced this version of subjectivity, that this position is not the only possible position; by exposing the perceptual/conceptual limitations that are hidden behind strategies of dominance and authority, the subject can be motivated to shift its position. However, as Husserl notes, the possibility of enlarging the scope of conscious-

Epistemological Crisis and the Phenomenalistic Subject

ness, of transforming subjectivity, depends upon an oscillation between the establishment of a centralized, mastery-oriented stance and the disruption of that mastery in a continuing, never completely realized process. If there is a universal human characteristic, in both Blake and in Husserl, it does not exist in some transcendental form but in the form of this persistent imposition of mastery on the part of a centralized subject who must engage all of its energies in defending itself against de-repressing an awareness of its limitations.

The problems associated with the production of precisely the transcendent central subject assumed by Damrosch and other commentators is thematized in the conclusion to *Jerusalem*. The end of the poem is often read as Albion's ascension to a transcendental state, but Plate 97, in which Albion becomes "fourfold," poses a set of problems for a reader who maintains a phenomenalistically central position and offers some possibilities for the transformation of self and of language that subvert—as well as reinscribe—reliance on that centrality.

The plate is divided roughly into thirds: the lower two-thirds of the plate comprise an image of a solitary figure, standing at the edge of darkness, his back to the viewer, carrying a bright sphere in his left hand; although a star and part of a crescent moon shine to his upper right, light beams seem to emanate from the figure to merge with the space on which the words are written. The following text occupies the upper third:

> Awake! Awake Jerusalem! O lovely Emanation of Albion
> Awake and overspread all Nations as in Ancient Time
> For lo: the Night of Death is past and the Eternal Day
> Appears upon our Hills: Awake Jerusalem.and come away
> So spake the Vision of Albion & in him so spake in my hearing
> The Universal Father Then Albion stretchd his hand into
>   Infinitude.
> And took his Bow. Fourfold the Vision for bright beaming
>   Urizen
> Layd his hand on the South & took a breathing Bow of carved
>   Gold
> Luvah his hand stretch'd to the East & bore a Silver Bow bright
>   shining
> Tharmas Westward a Bow of Brass pure flaming richly wrought
> Urthona Northward in thick storms a Bow of Iron terrible
>   thundering

> And the Bow is a Male & Female & the Quiver of the Arrows of
> Love.
> Are the Children of his Bow: a Bow of Mercy & Loving-kind-
> ness: laying
> Open the hidden Heart in Wars of mutual Benevolence Wars of
> Love
> And the Hand of Man grasps firm between the Male & Female
> Loves.
> And he Clothed himself in Bow & Arrows in awful state
> Fourfold
> In the midst of his Twenty-eight Cities each with his Bow
> breathing

Seen as a two-dimensional surface, the plate raises some immediate questions. The words describe Albion as four beings, but the figure in the plate has no visible face and only one head. In the text, each of Albion's four aspects carries a bow, yet the figure grasps a globe or sphere. The figure stands with its right knee bent and seems to be shielding his eyes with his right hand. What is the figure doing? What is its relation to the action described in the text? For that matter, who is this figure? The very two-dimensionality of this plate lures the viewing subject's interest as it obstructs its gaze, for it is not possible to see the face of this figure nor the object of its regard.

However, if the reader views the plate as a representational system for generating the illusion of three dimensions, the words will seem to hang suspended in the background of the space in which the figure stands. The words thus become an element in the scene of representation, a scene that now reveals itself as a *scene of reading*. The figure gazes into a distance occupied by the words of the poem. Furthermore, the perspective opened up by the plane on which the words are written implies that the living reader is oriented in a position below the reading figure. In other words, the central optic ray of the perspectival system—the ray that establishes the vanishing point of the scene represented and the viewpoint of the viewer in relationship to the figure—makes the figure "under-stand" the words, while the viewer "under-stands" the figure as reader.

The represented scene, therefore, reflects each moment of viewing the plate: the viewer may be identified with the figure as reader, and any viewer may take this place at the "outside" end of the central optic ray. But, of course, *any* words would serve that purpose

Epistemological Crisis and the Phenomenalistic Subject

Jerusalem, Plate 97. By permission of the Department of Printing and Graphic Arts, the Houghton Library, Harvard University.

for this scene. In fact, the relationship between viewer, figure, and text along this central ray creates an *obstacle* to vision rather than enlightenment. The focus along this ray for the living reader will always be the back of the figure's head, not the verbal text. Thus the central perspectival system obstructs the viewer's would-be comprehending gaze. The relationship between words, figure, and viewer along the central ray "says" that reading in a conventional sense, from a centralized viewpoint, succeeds only in reflecting the viewer's own lack of insight. The central moment defined by the central ray comments upon the viewer's actual state of—or lack of—vision *before* he or she has "read" the text to engage whatever transformations it might have to offer.

However, there is another perspectival system in this plate, one that displaces the focus of the optic rays in the central system just described. The focus of this perspective is the globe carried by the figure, the point at which the represented rays of light illuminating the verbal text merge. This is unexpected because one would assume that a literal rendering of the "light" of comprehension (or even natural light as it was understood in Blake's time) would show that light from the text would focus at the figure's eyes. Hence, the shift of the viewpoint from figure to globe institutes another perspectival system defined by the diagonal of the left leg of the figure and the rays perpendicular *to it*, rays from the globe leading to the verbal text, moon, and star (depending upon whether the ambiguous position of the globe is read as behind, beside, or in front of the figure). If the viewing subject could imagine itself positioned at the globe, looking along this new central optic ray, the figure itself would be seen in its outline, curved as a bow, echoed by the crescent moon at the vanishing point of that line. I take the incompleteness of the lunar crescent to refer to the limited range of vision that the reader has when positioned by the first perspectival system—the frame of the plate hides the rest of the moon, but it would appear in its complete crescent if the viewing subject were to "step inside," as it were, the scene to position itself along the central ray of the second perspectival system. What is more, if the figure could be viewed in its bow configuration, the odd lines marking the left back and buttock of the figure might stand out as a female head and torso, precisely at the spot where the bottom of a quiver would rest: as the

Epistemological Crisis and the Phenomenalistic Subject 95

poem states, "the Bow is a Male & Female & the Quiver of the Arrows of Love."[19]

The possibility of seeing the figure-as-bow depends upon the displacement of the viewing subject from its centralized viewpoint. The horizontal display of viewpoint and vanishing point on the surface of the plate destroys the spatial and temporal hierarchy imposed by the act of reading/viewing, producing instead an equivalence between objects that does not imply the mastery of the viewing subject. In effect, it transforms the depth dimension into a breadth dimension, undoing the perceptual limitation imposed by the phenomenalistic position of the centralized subject and removing the viewpoint that organizes space by reference to itself—in other words, creating a uniform space without a center. Merleau-Ponty has analyzed depth as

> tacitly equated with *breadth seen from the side*, and this is what makes it invisible.... What I call depth is in reality a juxtaposition of points, making it comparable to breadth. I am simply badly placed to see it. I should see it if I were in the position of a spectator looking on from the side.... In order to treat depth as breadth viewed in profile, in order to arrive at a uniform space, the subject must leave his place, abandon his point of view on the world, and think himself into a sort of ubiquity. For God, who is everywhere, breadth is immediately equivalent to depth.[20]

Merleau-Ponty calls depth the most "existential" of all dimensions because it arises from the perspective of the perceiving subject, not from the relations between objects. From the viewer's position objects are designated as "there" and the viewer "here." The "here/there" dimension becomes a "now/then" dimension, since the viewing subject serves as the reference for dividing time as well as space. Thus, by abandoning its possession of a central place and by varying its position, the subject can "create" space and time, changing the conditions of its existence.

19. Although Erdman does not identify the figure as the bow, he does suggest that the rays of light emanating from the globe "may be seen as an open left hand" (*The Illuminated Blake*, 376). This places the figure-as-bow in the palm of that hand: "And the Hand of Man grasps firm between the Male & Female Loves."
20. *The Phenomenology of Perception*, 255.

Although the displacement of the viewing subject makes depth and breadth equivalent because neither the spatial nor the temporal relationships between objects (or subjects) can be determined by reference to a single viewpoint, this displacement neither gives the subject access to a uniform space nor produces the equivalent of a Godlike omniperspective. The viewer must *repeatedly* shift point of view, subverting the centrality that reestablishes itself *with* each shift, a centrality that continues to assert its primacy over an objectified, externalized world. The subject always exists somewhere, even if that somewhere is not the "here" of a preceding moment; this means that at any moment, the subject will re-mark its centrality, and by extension, its (illusory) status as a determinate context that stabilizes or guarantees meaning.

The plate thematizes and dramatizes the necessity for a continual movement of displacement in order to subvert the bid for ultimate determinacy that attends the centralized subject's repression of its own limitations. Where the plate transforms a single imaged moment into a narrative of the displacement of the viewing subject, the verbal text presents a narrative sequence that results in an "Eternal" present. The speakers in the text gradually conflate into one voice, while the single viewer represented in the image can give way to a series of readers, each of whom must give up his or her point of view to read the plate insightfully. When the viewer learns this process of displacement, he or she may be inclined to give up a notion of consciousness as producing the meaning of the text through an original intentional act. For example, the reader is given a series of speaking subjects in Plate 97: "So spake the Vision of Albion & in him so spake in my hearing / The Universal Father." The lines create an ambiguity about which subject controls the discourse as well as about the relationship between these subjects, because the line break suggests that the Vision, Albion, and the narrative voice may all be part of the Universal Father. The very impossibility of ascribing a single authorial intention that would guarantee interpretation is dramatized here.

Blake's refusal to chain the text's productivity to the limitations of intentionality depends upon the reader's continuing attentiveness to the material supports of the text and to the mechanisms, such as perspectival systems and tropological functions, that it employs to create conditions of meaningfulness. Just as the picture can appear as a representation only to the extent that the material supports become invisible—the viewing subject doesn't see the picture as part of a referential representation if it is paying attention solely to the spots of light and dark on the page—so also does the linguistic text become referential only to the extent that its tropological function is ignored.[21] The illusion of transcendentally stabilized meaning emerges by means of the repression of the "tricks" by which referentiality appears as "natural"—tricks of perspective, tricks of light, tricks of tropes. The centralized subject produces a world of radical alienation and exploitative objectification insofar as it posits itself as the sole origin and determinant of the identity/meaning of the world and then represses its knowledge of that self-production by projecting its authority onto "nature." On this view, language has determinate meaning because nature itself guarantees referentiality. Blake's poem encourages the reader to undo that repression; by attending to the means by which the text creates its illusion of determinate meaning, the reader can use those means to transform perceptions, interpretations, and ultimately social relations.

The Typological Subject and the Ratio of Christ

Christian exegesis contains the traditional response to the limits of the spatiotemporally de-limited self. Seen from the perspective of Christian doctrine, the phenomenalistic self is not only insignificant but also most likely to be susceptible to rhetorical persuasion precisely because it lacks the eternal perspective obtained through a

21. In *Détruire la peinture*, Louis Marin explains that the "*invisibility* of the surface . . . is the condition of the possibility of the *visibility* of the represented world" (61, my translation). In this book, Marin discusses the conditions of representability in terms of the repression of the material supports of the painting.

reading of the Scriptures. On an Augustinian view, what appears to be subjectivity within a secular temporality in fact must be recuperated to its eternal aspect by particular or special rhetorical strategies, those that foreground language as Logos rather than those that mark the fallen languages of rhetoricity or "textuality." This position maps the body/spirit split onto a split in language itself. The body is phenomenality, limited by spatiotemporal constraints that finally are understood to be the products of a faulty perspective or the creations of a "defective" mind. The eternal aspect of every human identity can be recovered through the application of an exegetical paradigm that follows Augustinian hermeneutical assumptions and procedures. The typological method, then, supplies a determinate context within which to refigure the self-as-meaning. Without negating the importance of the flesh (which Christian doctrine asserts will also be resurrected), typology defends against the solipsism inherent in the position of the phenomenalistic self not by proposing the perpetual re-creation of different "selves" in different rhetorical or interpretive contexts, but by using Augustinian tropological strategies to interpret Christ's life as the *forma perfecta* of every life.[22]

In the traditional conception, the typological method takes as its founding assumption that the significance—and hence, the reality—of every subject's life derives from its relationship to the master narrative of Christ's life. One way to restate this position would be to say that it insists that subjects are constituted discursively, both psychologically, in that subjects are exhorted to model themselves consciously on Christ, and historically, in that subjects exist only as they reinscribe Christ's story. Blake's revision of the typological method

---

22. Thanks to Bishop Lowth and his contemporary literary historians, Blake's readers would have been able to find the term *typology* applied to a particular method of literary *construction* as well as to literary *interpretation*, for, as Lowth pointed out, later Old Testament figures are taken to be the types of earlier Old Testament figures, and, according to the Gospels, Jesus performed some of his actions *in order* to fulfill the prophecies of the Old Testament so as to make possible a text that conformed to the interpretive conventions for constituting sacred texts. See Paul J. Korshin's "The Development of Abstracted Typology in England, 1650–1820" for a discussion of the use of typology in Lowth, Warburton, Volney, Bryant, Butler, and other biblical commentators of that period. See also Frei's discussion of Herder's biblical interpretations in chapter 10 of *Eclipse*.

foregrounds the crucial importance of this insight concerning the discursive nature of subjectivity: in traditional typological exegesis this insight is employed in order to subsume particular narratives into one master narrative with the effect of negating the "experiential" reality or material history of individual subjects. By refusing to grant priority to a single narrative (Christ's, for example) over any other, Blake's "typology" maintains the typological subject's discursively constituted phenomenal reality without negating the particularity and the material efficacy of any individual life narrative.

Because typology proposes to collapse particular histories into one universal history, it is possible to comprehend Blake's revision of typological method by considering his rejection of the notion that history is an account of an actual event. Blake understands that most historians write their histories as though they had access to the ultimate "reality" that explains each event and its causal relations. His objection to the occulted embedding of historical events in an ideologically motivated causal framework does not reinstate the distinction between ontologically prior event and subsequent partial account so much as it emphasizes that the significance of each event does not inhere in its "actuality" but must always be deposited there by the interpreter:

> Act themselves alone are history and these are neither the exclusive property of Hume, Gibbon, nor Voltaire, Echard, Rapin, Plutarch, nor Herodotus. Tell me the Acts, O historian, and leave me to reason upon them as I please; away with your reasoning and your rubbish! all that is not action is not worth reading. Tell me the What; I do not want you to tell me the Why, and the How; I can find that out myself, as well as you can, and I will not be fooled by you into opinions, that you please to impose, to disbelieve what you think improbable or impossible (*Descriptive Catalogue*, E543–44)

The events of history detached from their causal explanations have no particular significance, except that given to them by the reader.[23]

[23]. It is typical of the commentary on Blake to read signifiers such as Locke, Bacon, Newton, Hume, and so forth as monovalent. Blake was a more subtle and generous reader of texts than his critics: it is obvious even in his most excoriating comments about Bishop Watson's arguments or Reynolds's theory of painting

Here as elsewhere, Blake clears a space for the interpretive activity of the reader, objecting to the imposition of an illusorily definite explanation of the events. Seen from this perspective, the events that every author will explain according to his or her own lights have no more significance (spiritual or otherwise) than any other events. Significance devolves from the act of reading/writing the causal narrative. This is true not only for so-called "actual historical" events, but for fictional events as well. An example of Blake's belief in the historical significance of fictional events appears in *The Ancient Britons* section of the *Descriptive Catalogue:*

> In the meantime he [Blake, referring to himself] has painted this Picture, which supposes that in the reign of that British Prince, who lived in the fifth century, there were remains of those naked Heroes, in the Welch Mountains; they are there now, Gray saw them in the person of his bard on Snowdon; there they dwell in naked simplicity; happy is he who can see and converse with them above the shadows of generation and death. The giant Albion, was Patriarch of the Atlantic, he is the Atlas of the Greeks, one of those the Greeks called Titans. The stories of Arthur are the acts of

---

that he is capable of distinguishing the valid from the invalid. Blake does not tend to dismiss thinkers wholeheartedly. What Blake might have objected to in Hume and Gibbon is the apparent reinscription in their work of a tolerant attitude toward monarchy. Blake's objection in the present instance to the historical writings of Hume and Gibbon could easily be applied to Whiggish historians, against whom Hume constructed his history. In the work of Whiggish historians, all events are accommodated to a progressivist teleology. What separates Hume from those historians, therefore, is not the fact of his causal explanation but the direction in which it tends. What Blake might have found congenial in Hume's work—both historical and philosophical—is the exposition of the role of local circumstances, political motivations, and conventional determinations of events and their significance. See, for example, Isaac Kramnick's exposition of Hume's anticontractarianism: "Hume went on to what is clearly the most devastating of all the skeptical repudiations of the notion of social contract. Society, he wrote in *Of the Origin of Government* and in *Of the Original Contract*, is the product of conventions and habit rather than of a rational decision on the part of any group to leave an inconvenient state of nature. Men obey their governments not from some ancestral promise of partnership in a social contract, but from the mere fact that a government has been established for a long time" ("Skepticism in English Political Thought: From Temple to Burke," 1643–44). As I argue in the next section, Blake's practice suggests a firmer adherence to the skeptical position regarding the nature of personal identity than Hume was inclined to take. Nonetheless, without Hume, it is difficult to see how either Blake or Kant would have taken up their respective concerns.

Albion, applied to a Prince of the fifth century, who conquered Europe, and held the Empire of the world in the dark age, which the Romans never again recovered. (E543)

Blake emphasizes the "historical" actuality of "those naked Heroes" as well as of Arthur and Albion, making no distinction between historical and fictional event. Blake's case for the historicity of fictional events becomes more credible when it is understood that he is arguing for the historical *efficacy* of fictional representations, their ability to alter the course of history, as well as for the fictiveness of all historiographical discourse.[24]

Tannenbaum suggests that this section of the *Catalogue* exemplifies Blake's use of typology—his conception of history as *kairos* as distinguished from *chronos*, "history as a number of moments containing divine and 'intemporal significance' from history based upon clock time." However, Blake not only makes it clear that an appeal to "the events themselves" will not establish a special status for one event as opposed to another (because every event derives its significance from the context in which it is regarded, the ideology invoked in order to maintain it) but his "typological" reading of Albion departs from traditional typological method as well. Tannenbaum explains that Blake applies "a paradigmatic figure to different times and places," a technique that he even employs "anachronistically" as when he asserts that the Hebrew Patriarchs were Druids. Albion, in Tannenbaum's view, is this "paradigmatic figure," just as Christ is in Biblical typology. Commenting on the validity of the substitution of Albion for Christ, Tannenbaum notes that the typological method as practiced by certain radical Higher Critics in Blake's time does not require the "actual" historical existence of Christ, nor does it insist upon the primacy of biblical texts as opposed to other myths. So far as this usage is concerned, there is no reason why Albion could not function typologically and nonidiosyncratically in Blake's work. Furthermore, Blake also insists on the mutuality of Albion

---

24. Again, I remind the reader of the risks of taking Blake's texts out of context to support "general principles" for interpreting Blake's work. The *Catalogue* descriptions, however, provide some perspectives on Blake's views of history that not only date from the period during which he was writing *Jerusalem* but also serve as reference points for much of the criticism on this topic.

and Christ within his work—that is, the mutuality of the giant Albion as the Human Form Divine and Christ as the "Eternal Body of Man" (*Laocoon*)—which supports Tannenbaum's proposal that Blake espouses the typological method.[25]

But this is typology of a peculiar sort. The Christocentric typological method depends for its effectiveness upon our knowledge of Christ's story, no matter whether we interpret literally, anagogically, or historically, so that we can apply it in relation to past events as a fulfillment and to future events as a prophecy. The events of Christ's life are models to be applied to the events of individual lives and temporal history in order to unveil their eternal significance. All events of human history are given their significance by reference to Christ's story.

Blake departs from this model: when he applies a given character's life story paradigmatically to a later event, it is that story—not the later event—which receives a new significance. In *Jerusalem* neither Christ's nor Albion's nor any other character's life serves as the *forma perfecta*, the interpretive standard. At the most basic level, Albion cannot be the *forma perfecta* that Christ is because the reader does not know his story and its "significant" events. In addition, biblical typology asserts that Christ understood that he functioned paradigmatically: for example, Jesus views Jonah as a type of the Son of Man because Jonah spent three days and three nights in the belly of the whale, just as Christ would spend three days and three nights in the tomb before his resurrection. None of *Jerusalem*'s characters understand themselves in this way. Furthermore, the biblical type functions positively (by reference to Christ, whose uniform positivity lends positive significance backwards, as it were), while Albion is frequently associated with negative characteristics. In chapter 2, for example, Albion speaks in an allusion to the God of book 3 of *Paradise Lost*:

> Albion replied: Go: Hand & Hyle! seize the abhorred friend: . . .
> Bring him to justice before heaven here upon London stone .
> All that they have is mine: from my free genrous gift
> They now hold all they have: ingratitude to me!
> To me their benefactor, calls aloud for vengeance deep.
> (Plate 42)

---

25. See Tannenbaum, *Biblical Tradition*, 87 and 95.

If Albion at this point is the *forma perfecta* of Milton's God, we must understand Milton's God as Blake did—as the incarnation of the ultimate vengeful Selfhood—and Albion as the signifier of some revisionary conception of typology.

"Therefore I print, nor vain my types shall be: / Heaven, Earth & Hell, henceforth shall live in harmony": these lines in the address "To the Public" imply that Blake employs some variant of the typological method in *Jerusalem*. The most obvious example of typology *as subject* in the poem, chapter 3's embedded story of Joseph and Mary, stages a critique of biblical typology on the grounds that the typological method establishes significance (and constrains narrativity) by attributing a priori and necessary status to what is essentially an arbitrary choice of type. Its very arbitrariness means that it easily becomes available for ideological ends that masquerade as truths. The search through texts and events for analogies will always succeed, not because there is in fact one paradigmatic story—a universal or eternal significance to which all stories refer—but because resemblance is a fundamental cognitive category. Not Jesus' life story but his method of constructing his life story as a fulfillment of analogous Old Testament figures is Blake's paradigm, for Jesus' procedure (or that of the authors of the Gospels) shows that narrative typology works backward to give significance to prior narratives and in so doing limits the significance of those narratives. Blake's critical tactic is to show that a typological method that seeks to establish a present or future significance based on past narratives cannot be limited, for the interpreter can never know which of the elements under consideration are to be compared.

The story of Joseph and Mary appears in Plate 61 as a framed tale within the story of Jerusalem herself, and it is presented directly as a story from which Jerusalem should draw significance for her own story:

> Behold: in the Visions of Elohim Jehovah. behold Joseph & Mary
> And be comforted O Jerusalem in the Visions of Jehovah Elohim
> She looked & saw Joseph the Carpenter in Nazareth & Mary His espoused Wife.

In these "Visions" Joseph is accusing Mary of being "a Harlot & an Adulteress." Mary does not deny the charge—"if I were pure. never could I taste the sweets / Of the Forgivess (sic) of Sins:"—but she insists that Joseph forgive her on the grounds that the "Maker . . . forgiveth Sins & calls again Her that is Lost / Tho She hates. he calls her again in love"—that is, on the grounds that Joseph should pattern himself after the *forma perfecta*, that their story should be the same as the story of the "Maker" and "Her that is Lost." Thus, within the first eight lines of this plate, the typological method is invoked as the ultimate guide to finding the proper significance of a life story.

At this point, however, things take a strange turn. Joseph reveals that "Her that is Lost" is in fact Jerusalem. In other words, Jerusalem is asked to understand that the story of Joseph and Mary furnishes the significance for her story, but the story of Joseph and Mary is the story of their learning to treat Jerusalem's story as a paradigm. With this stroke, Blake exposes the circular reasoning, post hoc analogizing, occulted premises, and arbitrary choices of typological readings. Then, Blake presents Jerusalem's difficulties with the typological method explicitly: Jerusalem rejects the analogy to Mary by continuing to consider herself unforgiven, but her rejection is not a consequence of her failure to recognize typological significance. Rather, it is a direct result of her recognition that typology furnishes too many possible analogies and no legitimate way to choose between them.

At the beginning of Plate 62 the voice that urged her to behold Joseph and Mary now exhorts her to substitute for her own life their life story's narrative: "Repose on me till the morning of the Grave. I am thy life." Within the space of nine lines, Jerusalem finds three possible types—the Bride, the Harlot, the Forgiven Adulteress—to satisfy this injunction:

> And wilt thou become my Husband O my Lord & Saviour?
> Shall Vala bring thee forth! shall the Chaste be ashamed also?
> I see the Maternal Line, I behold the Seed of Woman!
> Cainah. & Ada & Zillah & Naamah Wife of Noah.
> Shuahs daughter & Tamar & Rahab the Canaanites:
> Ruth the Moabite & Bathsheba of the daughters of Heth
> Naamah the Ammonite, Zibeah the Philistine. & Mary
> These are the Daughters of Vala, Mother of the Body of death
> But I thy Magdalen behold thy Spiritual Risen Body

If she chooses the analogy of the Bride, "repose on me" implies her marriage to the "Lord & Saviour." But "repose on me" could also imply an extramarital sexual relationship, reinscribing her identity as Harlot. Or, the negation of the body implied in the Forgiven Adulteress paradigm, reappearing here in the line, "But I, thy Magdalen, behold thy Spiritual Risen Body," could be signaled in the voice's claim "I am thy life." Jerusalem's efforts to understand the significance of her story by reference to some given or fixed pattern ("I am thy life") do not succeed because she would have to have already known which events and interpretations of her life were significant in order to find the appropriate precursor text. Traditional typology entails this tautology while denying it: Blake's alternative is to use the disseminative possibilities inherent in the typological method against itself.

Jerusalem's vacillation about the significance of her own story, her inability to find one paradigmatic story that will stabilize her own history and the history that she might engender, has consequences for the terms in which we will read the presumptively benevolent and transcendental divinity of the voice who bids her use typology to reconstruct her self. The presupposition that the voice has transcendental perspective or benevolent purposes is called into question not only by Mary's insight that Christian doctrine has to *create* sinners in order to have a reason for pity and forgiveness, not only by Jerusalem's discovery that the voice's assertions can situate her with the damned as well as the forgiven, and not only by the explicit threat to Jerusalem of "Repose on me till the morning of the Grave. I am thy life," but also by the possibility that Jerusalem's life constitutes the life of the voice rather than the other way around.

Although Blake seems to approve of readings of the Scriptures and other works that encouraged their application as exempla, his texts continually resist the occulted premises of typology. In the same year as the review of Nitsch's interpretation of Kant appeared, so did Bishop Watson's diatribe against Paine, to which Blake responded:

> I cannot concieve the Divinity of the <books in the> Bible to consist either in who they were written by, or at what time, or in the historical evidence which may be all false in the eyes of one man & true in the eyes of another, but in the Sentiments & Examples,

which, whether true or Parabolic, are Equally useful as Examples given to us of the perverseness of some & its consequent evil & the honesty of others & its consequent good . . . None can doubt the impression which he recieves from a book of Examples. If he is good he will abhor wickedness in David or Abraham if he is wicked he will make their wickedness an excuse for his & so he would do by any other book. ("Annotations," E618)

In biblical typology the value of the event proposed as the paradigm is known in advance, while in Blake's view that value changes with each reader, with each context. The consequence of this distinction is revealed as a displacement of the metaphysical guarantees that supposedly underwrite the biblical hermeneutical project as well as the epistemological projects of the late eighteenth century.

By disseminating rather than reducing stories, Blake's method creates a "paradigm" of the Human Form Divine that sidesteps the oppressive effects of regarding one story as universal. Hence Los is both correct and incorrect when he chastises the Sons of Albion:

> Los cries: No Individual ought to appropriate to Himself
> Or to his Emanation. any of the Universal Characteristics
> Of David or of Eve. of the Woman. or of the Lord,
> Of Reuben or of Benjamin, of Joseph or Judah or Levi
> Those who dare appropriate to themselves Universal Attributes
> Are the Blasphemous Selfhoods & must be broken asunder.
> . . . .
> So Los cried in the Valleys of Middlesex in the Spirit of
>   Prophecy
> While in Selfhood Hand & Hyle & Bowen & Skofeld
>   appropriate
> The Divine Names: seeking to Vegetate the Divine Vision
> In a corporeal & ever dying Vegetation & Corruption
> Mingling with Luvah in One. they become One Great Satan
>   (Plate 90)

The appropriation of universal attributes as though they furnished any given individual with an eternally universal significance is wrong, but neither Los nor the narrative voice sees that the "Divine Names" do not have a privileged status with regard to the Sons of Albion. Within chapter 3, Blake reveals the difficulties posed by the reductive, consuming vision of the typological method: all narrative is susceptible to reinterpretation according to some preexisting pattern, and we not only have to choose among a number of possible patterns but also have to repress the a priori standard of evaluation we use to choose one narrative as having more morally instructive value than another.

We can fathom the problem with the typological method from a Blakean point of view, for even in its broadest usage it proposes that all history be viewed in terms of one story and that Christ, in the words of the epigraph to Part 1, Section 1, functions merely as a "Ratio" of comparison. It is just as important to note, however, that this description serves equally well as a characterization of the strategies of repression that enable ideological functions. As Althusser notes, ideologies have no history: an ideology articulates a past onto a present by repressing any conflictual elements. It treats all time as eternal time, creating the impression that a particular, historically delimited, defined, and deployed "value"—which in itself may be used for exploitive or oppressive purposes—exists universally and benevolently. The repression of elements of difference and narrativity function to create this illusion that ideology has no history by repressing the history that is the ideology's own.[26] Furthermore, the Christ of traditional typology is the medium in and through which individuals understand who they are and what their function is, a kind of pre-Althusserian formulation of "ideology" understood as "a 'representation' of the imaginary relationship of individuals to their real conditions of existence."

The "One Great Satan" of the reductive and consuming project described by Los would work equally well as a description of the ideological function Christ serves in traditional Biblical typology or as a description of the occulted ideological premises of the philosophical programs of Blake's era. It is perhaps serendipitous that the expositions of Kant to which Blake had access describe reason in these terms as well:

> Being convinced, that reason must either in part or wholly constitute [the capacity by which we are enabled to know things], Mr.

---

26. See Althusser, "Ideology and Ideological State Apparatuses." I call the reader's attention to David Gross's splendid article " 'Mind-Forg'd Manacles': Hegemony and Counter-Hegemony in Blake" for a discussion of the usefulness of applying a Gramscian notion of ideological hegemony to Blake's work.

> Kant immediately perceived the necessity of previously inquiring into the nature of this faculty. 'Reason,' observes Mr. N[itsch], 'considered in its most limited and definite operation . . . is that faculty which concludes or acquires knowledge by *conclusion*; and a conclusion is the perception of the agreement or disagreement of two ideas, by comparing them with a third.' 'But,' says Mr. N., p. 34, 'grant these definitions to be correct, and it will follow, that reason, so far from knowing any thing can of itself know nothing. For how can a mere concluding faculty, as it has been just described, give knowledge, when it supposes ideas, of which knowledge is composed, as necessary to the exercise of its functions.'[27]

Kant is implicitly objecting to the difference- and temporality-suppressing character of reason. The occulted petitio principii that Kant and/or his explicator note in this description of reason serves as a fundamental objection to the occulting of the a priori and ideologically motivated significance of Christ's life that, when viewed from a Blakean perspective, shows that Christ is nothing more than a standard of comparison, a mechanically produced ratio. The answer to Kant's question was given by Hume and other radical skeptics, although it appears nowhere in Kant: social discourses and practices, "custom" and tradition—ideological constructs and disseminations—give reason its standard of evaluation. Blake's response emerges in his analysis of the "subject of discourse" as a means to subvert unfounded metaphysics while sidestepping the dangers of solipsism.

Blake's Antimetaphysics and the Subject of Discourse

Typological readings are essentially antinarratival, reducing all stories to one story, inscribing a transcendental subjectivity in the space of particular historical identities. Because *Jerusalem* does not present a

---

27. "Nitsch's *Introductory View*," 13.

straightforward chronological narrative, many commentators draw the conclusion that Blake regards narrative as an inherently unsatisfactory literary mode.[28] Yet even the apocalyptic conclusion to the poem, where one might reasonably expect a departure from narrative principles, reinstates narrativity as the basis of human existence:

> All Human Forms identified even Tree Metal Earth & Stone. all
> Human Forms identified. living going forth & returning
>   wearied
> Into the Planetary lives of Years Months Days & Hours reposing
> And then Awaking into his Bosom in the Life of Immortality.
> And I heard the Name of their Emanations they are named
>   Jerusalem
>   The End of The Song
>   of Jerusalem
>   (Plate 99)

The apparent recourse to a transcendent and eternal state, the Life of Immortality, in this conclusion to the poem needs to be explored. What is the status of "divinity" in the poem? And what, consequently, are the valences Blake's text gives to narratives and to subjects? Blake's poem is resolutely antimetaphysical, the apparent allusion to a Christian redemption in this conclusion notwithstanding. This moment in the text *is* redemptive, but only if it is recognized for what it is: the last opportunity for the reader to identify the extent to which ideological assumptions appear to produce "natural" or inevitable interpretations. The reader has been encouraged to read tropologically to recognize the limits that occulted institutionalized significations and values place on the "perception" of the world. The conclusion of Plate 98 makes the exhortation to tropological reading explicit:

> Where is the Covenant of Priam.the Moral Virtues of the
>   Heathen
> Where is the Tree of Good & Evil that rooted beneath the cruel
>   heel

---

28. In this poem, narration is a fundamental category of analysis: without an ideology of narrative *as* causally motivated, temporally coherent discourse, the reader would never discover the limitations such an ideology imposes—and hence would have no reason to note the ways in which that ideology is already at work organizing the world, the text, and the self.

> Of Albions Spectre the Patriarch Druid! where are all his Human Sacrifices
> For Sin in War & in the Druid Temples of the Accuser of Sin: beneath
> The Oak Groves of Albion that coverd the whole Earth beneath his Spectre
> Where are the Kingdoms of the World & all their glory that grew on Desolation
> The Fruit of Albions Poverty Tree when the Triple Headed Gog-Magog Giant
> Of Albion Taxed the Nations into Desolation & then gave the Spectrous Oath

This "Cry from all the Earth" suggests that we ask the questions that will mark the places where absolute determinations of signification have been permitted to function as though they were given or natural. These are tropological questions, not because the Covenant of Priam has disappeared, nor because oppositional categories that are products of training rather than essential components of the world, such as good and evil, cease to function, but because the questions direct the reader to look for the places in his or her own discourse (philosophy, religion, system of social relations) where he or she has subscribed to that covenant, erected the Tree of Good & Evil, judged everyone according to one law or produced all meaning according to one eternal or universal context. Once these questions have been answered, the reader can then identify how to engage those ideological constructs tropologically.

For such a reader—a reader who can mark his or her own phenomenalistic limitations and ideological presuppositions—space and time, as well as the form of social relations, will vary with milieu, motivation, and historical circumstance. Subjectivity itself varies *as* a "subject of discourse," both because the subject is discursively (but not monologically) constituted and because discursivity is the means by which the subject enacts its (variable) subjectivity:

> And they conversed together in Visionary forms dramatic which bright
> Redounded from their Tongues in thunderous majesty, in Visions
> In new Expanses. creating exemplars of Memory and of Intellect
> Creating Space. Creating Time
>
> (Plate 98)

Blake's Antimetaphysics and the Subject of Discourse 111

The reading subject who has "exercised" its intellect with the contextual displacements, tropological potentialities, and disseminated authorities of the poem may well understand its final lines as calling for one further identification, the identification that sees past the limitations of conventional line breaks and of traditional Christian narrative to read "reposing / And then Awaking into his Bosom in the Life of Immortality" as a phrase in apposition to "all / Human Forms identified, living going forth & return wearied / Into the Planetary lives of Years Months Days & Hours." The "Life of Immortality" is precisely the generation of variations of subjectivity that extend from the limit of contraction of the atomistic individual's obsessive remarking of the opposition between "living" subjects and "stonified" objects to the movement from "Eternity to Eternity . . . as One Man." Each of these states—and the intermediate stages of identification and variation—has its advantages and disadvantages; all that Blake puts out of play is the absolute hierarchical valuation of these states, which would follow from the imposition of a unitary metaphysical standard.

When Jehovah speaks "Terrific from his Holy Place," the narrator sees the world as textuality: he

> saw the Words of the Mutual Covenant Divine
> . . . with living Creatures starry & flaming
> With every Colour. Lion.Tyger.Horse.Elephant.Eagle
>   Dove.Fly.Worm
> And the all wondrous Serpent clothed in gems & rich array
>   Humanize
>
> (Plate 98)

The inscription of "divinity" as a pluralized textuality corresponds to the "humanization" of oppressive metaphysics that occurs when we recognize that the phenomenalistically oriented self exists in complicity with the oppressive metaphysics of absolute authority: in both cases the "natural" guarantee of centrality is revealed to be a trick of tradition or linguistic convention, of ideological imposition.

One plate in the poem provides a particularly compelling analysis of this complicity and the discursive or narratival constitution of subjectivity. The second plate of chapter 2 (Plate 29) appears as the fifth plate (Plate 33) in the equally authoritative alternative ordering of the text; the plates that precede this plate are quite different. Thus, this plate initiates a disruption of any ideology of reading that depends upon assumptions of causality, telos, and unity. This plate demonstrates how narrative processes naturalize themselves, producing the illusion of metaphysical presence and transcendental subjectivity. In this reading of the plate, I position the text within an eighteenth-century conceptual field demarcated by the complex relations between positivism and skepticism, the same complexities that led Kant to undertake the *Critiques*. I do not argue that Blake's work constitutes an endorsement of the "systems" of either positivism or skepticism; I do argue that the systems provide, particularly in the Comteam and Humean versions, an analysis that disallows metaphysical legitimations, even if neither follows the implications of this delegitimation of metaphysical priority to the point of deconstructing the primacy, respectively, of the ontologically "real" or of "universal human nature." Both ultimately reinscribe metaphysics by recourse to "observable phenomena" or "universal moral law." But Blake does carry out that deconstruction in *Jerusalem* in an analytics of narrativity that reveals how narratives repress uncertainties about ends and origins by summoning up an ontologically transcendent "reality" to which the narrative supposedly "refers." At the same time, it shows how the vexed epistemological status of the subject in eighteenth-century moral philosophy receives an illusory grounding through the production of narratives that serve as "stable" or "coherent" memories of a "continuous" self-identity.

Plate 29/33 of *Jerusalem*, like so much of the poem, encourages the search for transcendent authority: the stages of this search reenact the "creation" of God, nature, gender, self, history, and narrative itself as sites of the metaphysically "real." To appreciate the complexity of Blake's achievement in subverting all metaphysical claims, it is helpful to begin with the conventional assumptions about narrative teleology and determinate meaning that constitute what Blake seems to believe is the dominant ideology of reading of his day, one predicated upon the assumptions of "Single vision." I follow Donald Ault's method in "Re-Visioning *The Four Zoas*" (later expanded into *Narrative Unbound*) of attending to the different interpretations enabled by syntactical and grammatical peculiarities of the text as well as by the apparently random marks of the page. Ault characterizes the worldview that gives ontological priority to external objects, rejecting the possibility that "the way something is perceived constitutes its being or reality," as corresponding to the "Single vision" that Blake despises. "Single vision and Newtons sleep" refers to the presupposition that behind all the partial and distorted subjective impressions we have of the world, there exists a unified, teleologically consistent, and complete "actual" world. These assumptions comprise the grounding presuppositions of a traditional ideology of reading as well.[29]

However, that ideology presumes a "beginning," a concept radically challenged by Blake's indeterminate text. So I begin with a rupture—at the opening of the second/fifth plate of the second chapter:

> Turning his back to the Divine Vision, his Spectrous
> Chaos before his face appeard: an Unformd Memory
> Then spoke the Spectrous Chaos to Albion darkning cold
> From the back & loins where dwell the Spectrous Dead

Syntactically, these lines set up various and conflicting identifications. The first pronoun, *his*, does not have an antecedent (again, this plate has two separate "previous" plates, one focused on Albion and one on Los). In reading the pronouns within the context of these lines, as candidates for their referents become available, the following questions arise: Do the first two pronouns refer to the same entity, in which case, ought we to equate Divine Vision and Spectrous Chaos, an equivalence suggested by the potentially appositive comma? The third *his* appears to clear up this momentary confusion: by turning his back, whoever "he" is leaves the Divine Vision behind and confronts the Spectrous Chaos. Yet if the first two lines suggest these relatively clear spatial relations, what does it mean that the Spectrous Chaos speaks to Albion "from the back & loins"? Is the Spectrous Chaos speaking from its *own* back and loins? Do

---

29. Paul Mann's essay *"The Book of Urizen* and the Horizon of the Book" initiates a critique of "textuality" as an idealized counterterm to the deterministic reading practices that constitute a conventional ideology of reading. I extend his critique in the following section.

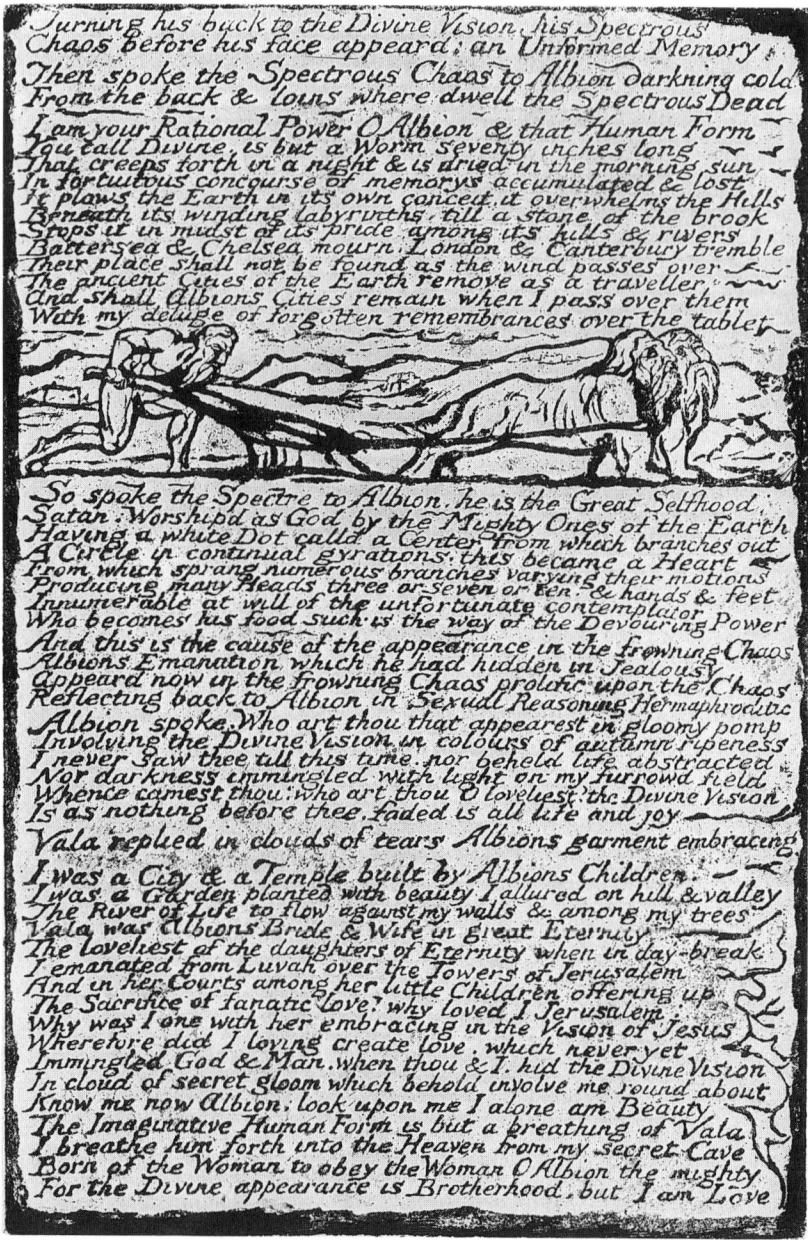

Jerusalem, Plate 29/33. By permission of the Department of Printing and Graphic Arts, the Houghton Library, Harvard University.

"Unformd" chaoses *have* backs and loins? Or, if these are Albion's back and loins, "where dwell the Spectrous Dead," does this place the Divine Vision in the same site as the Spectrous Dead? Are the third and fourth lines an enjambment, which would suggest that the Spectrous Chaos is not speaking to Albion's face but to his back and loins and which would further suggest that the spatial relations of the first two lines have been compromised? If the Spectrous Chaos appears *before* "his" face but speaks *from* Albion's back and loins, then perhaps Albion is not the referent for the pronouns in the first lines, in which case that pronoun has no evident antecedent. Maybe Albion is "darkning cold" in his own back and loins? Or is it the Spectrous Chaos who is "darkning cold"? What exactly is this "Unformd Memory"—does it refer to the entire narrative of someone turning his back and confronting the Spectrous Chaos, or does it suggest that the Spectrous Chaos itself is an Unformd Memory? In an evident attempt to stabilize some of this uncertainty, the editor places a period at the end of the second line, but no such mark exists in many of the printings. Perhaps, then, the Unformd Memory is somehow speaking/ producing the Spectrous Chaos, or the Spectrous Chaos is speaking/producing the Unformd Memory.

In taking these instabilities seriously, I argue that the first four lines articulate a problem and a strategy that will recur throughout the plate. The undecidable identifications of "the Divine Vision, his Spectrous / Chaos" are distinguished by reference to a geography that itself appears to be ontologically prior to the "events" of these lines; this geography seems to supply the spatiotemporal matrix that enables causal action. However, the "origin" of this geography (that which provides all the spatial markers) is the triply iterated, underdetermined pronoun *his*—a nonlocatable possessive function that demarcates not only the spatial coordinates of "in front of"/"behind" but also the temporal coordinates of "before"/"after." In fact, the spatialized "before" operates a temporal "afterwards": does his Spectrous Chaos appear in front of his face after he turned his back to the Divine Vision, or does he turn his back to the Divine Vision/Spectrous Chaos at a time before his face appeared? This spatiotemporal crossing disrupts the unity of "his"; no matter how nebulous the identity to which that pronoun might refer, the spatial and temporal relations of the first two lines leave open the possibility that there is more than one "his." The creation of space and time as a function of a possessive linguistic function—a function that is exposed as multiple precisely where it proposes its univocity—corresponds to Blake's critique of the perceptual operations of a centralized subjectivity and to the horizon produced by the perceptual limitation of such a subjectivity.

Once that subjectivity is decentered or deconstructed as being a trace of operations of ordering and mastery, once its disorganized features emerge, the plate reinscribes that disorganization into both a narrative structure and a centralized subject. As "an Unformd Memory," the opening line and a half of the plate loses its claims to represent a stable, ordered reality, but the text undercuts the subversive aspects of this insight by placing it in "memory," thereby at once stipulating to its disorder *and* referencing a before and after at another site.

Late eighteenth-century philosophy provides the terms Blake uses here to speculate on the role of memory and causality in the construction of personal identity; Hume so effectively expounds the skeptical position that Kant is moved to construct a counterargument. In Hume we find the skeptical argument that there are no epistemologically valid grounds to support a rational attribution of the continuity of self-identity, as well as an admission that his analysis contains an inexplicable contradiction. Hume begins with causality:

> [A subject encountering a continual succession of objects or events following one another], he would not, at first, by any reasoning, be able to reach the idea of cause and effect; since the particular powers, by which all natural operations are performed, never appear to the sense; nor is it reasonable to conclude, merely because one event, in one instance, precedes another, that therefore the one is the cause, the other the effect . . . [upon further experience of the same succession] he immediately infers the existence of one object from the appearance of the other. Yet he has not, by all his experience, acquired any idea of knowledge of the secret power by which the one object produces the other; nor is it, by any process of reasoning, he is engaged to draw this inference . . . There is some other principle which determines him to form such a conclusion. This principle is *custom* or *habit*.[30]

30. *Enquiry Concerning Human Understanding*, section 5, part 1, 42–43.

Just as we subjectively attribute *causality* to what is merely the objective experience of constant conjunction, so we assume that independent mental perceptions are connected and call that connection *identity:*

> Memory, by raising up images of past perceptions, produces a relation of resemblance among our perceptions: and the imagination is thus carried more easily along the chain, so that the chain appears to be a continued and persistent object. . . . Once given memory, our perceptions are linked by association in the imagination, and we attribute identity to what is in fact an interrupted succession of related perceptions. . . . Hence memory is to be accounted the chief source of the idea of personal identity.[31]

In Hume's account memory guarantees the integrity of identity, but it is an unsatisfactory warrant. Hume complains in the *Treatise of Human Nature* that he cannot "explain the principles that unite our successive perceptions in our thought or consciousness . . . In short, there are two principles which I cannot render consistent; nor is it in my power to renounce either of them viz. *that all our distinct perceptions are distinct existences*, and *that the mind never perceives any real connection among distinct existences*"[32] Memory is the analogue in the sphere of mental operations to causality in the sphere of physical operations—a subjective attribution, a fabrication underwritten by personal habit and social custom. Thus, for Hume, causal connections between physical or mental operations are narrative constructions.

Kant's analysis of man's freedom from the constraints of causal, experiential conditions served as the fundamental move in his creation of a transcendental position, a position isolated from empirical reality, from other subjects, and from any ideologically constructed reality. This move also entails a corresponding negation of the possibility that memory acts to preserve some external reality, whether that reality is construed as ontological or as ideologically produced. Hume rejects causality for a different reason, on account of our inability to *know* with certainty that the impressions of a self that exist over time are in fact essentially conjoined or derive from a core

31. Frederick Copleston, *A History of Philosophy*, book 2, vol. 5, 303.
32. *Treatise*, book 1, part 4, section 6, 262.

identity. For Hume and the other associationists, memory is a critical faculty—not because it insures a relationship to actual reality, but because it provides the illusion of identity. Identity and causality are customary constructs, enabled by a memory that does not necessarily accurately represent reality but which provides a form, structure, or relation where none need be present. In Hume, memory can be both formed and unformed: in the sense that it need not be shaped by experience of an actual world (and in that sense may *transcend* experience) it is unformed; but in the sense that it gives a form not empirically given, it is formed, or forming. The invocation of an "unformed" memory to mark the boundaries of a description in which identity and causality are problematized refers both to a critique of the Kantian repression of the realm of history and the role of ideology in providing a priori values or "real" givens *and* to an acknowledgment of the defensive role that conceptions of memory play in Hume's struggle to follow and suppress his own skepticism.

By invoking "memory" as a problematized cause and guarantee of identity at this moment in the plate, Blake rearticulates the fractured metaphysics of transcendental subjectivity and productively reinscribes the Humean problem. The indeterminate causal relations and identifications of the first lines would be seen on Hume's analysis as an accurate representation of the problem of ascribing continuity and integrity to personal identity based on an assumption of causality. But the Humean objection to relying on memory as a guarantee of personal identity seems to be defended against by this move to a metalevel, an evocation of a consciousness capable of bridging those discontinuities. These next lines propose "Albion" as a discrete identity, distinguishing him (however illegitimately) from the incomprehensible, nonlocatable, and somehow threatening "Spectrous Chaos," as though consolidating the strategic defenses of transcendental idealism against Hume's representation of subjectivity as discontinuity, disruption, and disintegration. Yet, as we see in these next lines as well as in the next passage of the plate, the distinction between Albion and Spectrous Chaos is illegitimate and the strategic appeal to memory inadequate to fend off the possibility that the ground on which the autonomous, centralized subject has been erected will be undermined.

The failure of this strategy to defend against the possibility that the Spectrous Chaos and the Divine Vision (or Albion) might occupy the same site—that they might indeed exist in complex relations to each other that are not comprehended by a simple antithesis based on a stable topography or a causal temporality—is signified by the emergence of a new entity occupying that same site, "the Spectrous Dead." The text, in a move analogous to the displacement, stipulation, and recuperation enacted at the end of line two, responds to the ambiguity of these identifications in the next section:

> I am your Rational Power O Albion & that Human Form
> You call Divine, is but a Worm seventy inches long
> That creeps forth in a night & is dried in the morning sun
> In fortuitous concourse of memorys accumulated & lost
> It plows the Earth in its own conceit. it overwhelms the Hills
> Beneath its winding labyrinths. till a stone of the brook
> Stops it in midst of its pride among its hills & rivers
> Battersea & Chelsea mourn. London & Canterbury tremble
> Their place shall not be found as the wind passes over
> The ancient Cities of the Earth remove as a traveller
> And shall Albions Cities remain when I pass over them
> With my deluge of forgotten remembrances over the tablet

This passage reproduces and enacts the gestures of the opening four lines of this plate in at least three ways. First, both passages have undecidable enunciative origins. Although we may be tempted to treat the source of the first four lines as a kind of narrative authority in the tradition of epic poetry, its claims to such authority are compromised by its failure to elucidate time, space, and identity in a straightforward way. And, despite the apparent shift to direct discourse in the next passage, these subsequent lines also emerge from an undecidable source, an undecidability apparently stabilized only *after* the speech. Here, as noted above, these lines could be said by "the Spectrous Chaos to Albion" or by "an Unformd Memory" articulating the Spectrous Chaos, in which case the passage itself becomes the equivalent of a Spectrous Chaos.

Secondly, in this passage as well as in the first four lines of the poem, the key problem of identifying divinity reappears. Here the speaker taunts Albion with misidentifying the human as divine: "that Human Form / You call Divine, is but a Worm." Yet in a construction reminiscent of the opening of the plate, the syntax of the first lines of this passage permits multiple identifications: "I am your Rational Power O Albion & that Human Form / You call Divine . . ." The text encourages this second reading of multiple identifications—including the possibility that the Rational Power is "that Human Form / You call Divine"—both through the ambiguous mark read by editors Erdman and Bloom as a comma (it could also be a period) and by the ampersand, a punctuation mark Blake had just used to indicate coordination rather than antithesis. The structure of this ambiguous syntax produces the conditions of continuous revision concerning the identities of these "beings": what results, then, is no method for creating determinacy but a shifting background of syntactical relations that serve minimally to subvert all appeals to determinacy, appeals that the text itself emphasizes as inaccurately denominated transcendentals. Like the first four lines, this segment of the plate does not accord "divinity" the status of a transcendent signifier.

Third, in another gesture analogous to the opening of the plate, the speaker deconstructs the metaphysical bases for a transcendent subjectivity, apparently setting up a critique of associationist/empiricist versions of identity as being based on memory: "fortuitous concourse of memorys accumulated & lost" reiterates the deconstructive potential of the Humean and Hartleian concepts of self. Nothing in the associationism on which both Hartley and Hume rely demands that the product of a psyche formed on associationist principles will be coherent or even self-knowledgeable.[33] Identity is nothing more than memory, a notoriously impotent faculty, producing nothing other than the illusion of integrity and continuity and subject to the vicissitudes of experience, including the possibility of memory loss. What if a "deluge of forgotten remembrances" washes over "the tablet"? Consciousness can become a tabula rasa at any moment because nothing in fact guarantees the continuity of memory. Memory does not retain impressions of actual experience but is itself a complex of fabrications and omissions, a complexity underscored by the causally indeterminate phrase "forgotten remembrances." Such a faculty provides no basis for a psychology of coherent selfhood.

33. For a discussion of Hume's deconstruction of causality as it bears on associationist approaches to subjectivity, see Copleston's *History*, book 2, vol. 5, especially 278–88.

After this speech, as if in response to these shifting identities, subversions of authority, and dispersals of consciousness, the narrative voice steps in with a "definitive" identification of the speaker, an identification that permits us to reject the problems raised by the preceding passage as products of a "mistaken" being:

> So spoke the Spectre to Albion. he is the Great Selfhood
> Satan: Worshipd as God by the Mighty Ones of the Earth
> Having a white Dot calld a Center from which branches out
> A Circle in continual gyrations. this became a Heart
> From which sprang numerous branches varying their motions
> Producing many Heads three or seven or ten. & hands & feet
> Innumerable at will of the unfortunate contemplator
> Who becomes his food such is the way of the Devouring Power

Whatever the complexities of identification prior to this point in the text, the confusion seems to clear up with the naming of the speaker as "the Spectre," although the next lines provide several, conflicting names—the Great Selfhood, Satan, God—each of which, thanks to the ambiguous referent of "he is," could be ascribed either to the Spectre or to Albion. As in the first two sections of the plate, "someone" is always commingling the divine, the spectral/satanic, the human. Once again the problem of identifying "divinity" emerges, and in its efforts to assert its own authority, this voice produces *as a character* (Satan, the Great Selfhood) the source of the confusion, projecting him backwards and forwards in time to give him a location suspiciously like the classical definition of God—a circle whose circumference is everywhere and whose center is nowhere.

In fact, it is the narrative voice that has made its bid for godlike omniscience.[34] In other words, the term *Spectrous Chaos* describes a narrative situation in which spatiotemporal relations and identities are indeterminate and therefore can be used as material to be shaped

---

34. See Stuart Peterfreund's "Argument as Art, Argument as Science." Peterfreund argues that Blake regards Newton's denial of responsibility for creating the hypothesis of an inaccessible, centralized, authoritative God—a hypothesis on which Newton's physical description of the universe depends—as producing a "fallen" universe, a reified nature, and a humanity alienated from nature and from itself. Attributing to God a view of nature that is in fact his own construction, Newton erases himself in order to position God "invisible, at the center of a universe composed of very visible, very dead, atomistic matter" (215).

by rhetorical processes (such as definition, exclusion, the creation of oppositions) and strategies for establishing legitimacy in the absence of transcendental guarantees of authority. By responding to this situation through the imposition of determinate relations, identities, and causation, the narrative voice mobilizes a number of traditional assumptions, values, and operations about narrative itself that dramatize what until this point in the plate have been seen as formal textual properties, such as ambiguous syntax. The bid for determinate order only *reproduces* the conditions it seeks to alleviate. The narrative voice attempts to assume the position of the divine while it describes as illegitimate the same usurpations on the part of the character it created but disclaims responsibility for creating ("Having a white Dot calld a Center . . . this became a Heart"). In the process, it alleges that the Spectre/Selfhood/Satan (otherwise known as God) produced the conditions of multiple identities with unclear physical boundaries *after* some "original" situation of clarity. This accusation personifies, provides an origin for, and condemns as "satanic" the incoherences of plural and incommensurable narrative possibilities:

> From which sprang numerous branches varying their motions
> Producing many Heads three or seven or ten. & hands & feet
> Innumerable . . .

At the same time, however, the text disorganizes the causal logic and identifications it has just set up, for this multiplex textual situation arises, it claims, as a function of or consequence of the "will of the unfortunate contemplator," the one who purports merely to be describing or observing processes outside itself but that it is, in fact, producing—that is, as a function of the kind of subjectivity represented by the narrative voice itself.

These lines are separated from the preceding speech by the plate's only illustration, a compressed horizontal space extending across the breadth of the page in which a man is crouched over a plow harnessed to "two" lions with men's faces in a valley below some low hills. Apparently an image of the "Human Form" that "plows the Earth in its own conceit, it overwhelms the Hills," the image divides the speech of the Spectre from that of the narrative voice, thereby masking the similarities of the attitudes in each. What the Spectre attributes to the Human Form, the narrative voice attributes to the Spectre, and both attributions could equally well describe the activities of the narrative voice itself. It is significant that the beast pulling the plow is indeterminately "double": it has two heads but only one body. The division of the plate enacted by this illustration also creates an indeterminate doubling of Spectre and narrative voice. The process of division and the positing of actions by autonomous entities as explanations for complex, implicate processes is, in this plate, always a function of a centralized Selfhood, arrogating to itself all authority, knowledge, and truth. To accept the illustration as merely an explanatory image of the plowing described in the Spectre's speech—the significance of which is limited to its referential dimension—would be to enact the division of the plate into separate segments that reproduces the spatial, causal, and deterministic logic the plate itself subverts. Plowing is both divisive and productive: it devolves from "conceit" but it is not an unambiguous sign of the mastery of the selfhood.

The story of Satan's generation of multiplicity that this narrative voice tells, then, projects as external to itself and as prior to its own operations a "reality" it simply reports. But the text continues to comment upon the inadequate metaphysical grounding of this narrative strategy. In the next lines, the narrative voice "reveals" the "cause" of the instabilities it claims the Spectre has engendered:

> And this is the cause of the appearance in the frowning Chaos
> Albions Emanation which he had hidden in Jealousy
> Appeard now in the frowning Chaos prolific upon the Chaos
> Reflecting back to Albion in Sexual Reasoning Hermaphroditic

In order for the validity of the narrative about the Spectre's conflictual productions to hold, it has to "devour" alternative causalities. This process, we might say, actually is the "way of the Devouring Power": the exclusion or negation of these possibilities. Therefore, we can read these lines as saying that the "cause of the appearance in the frowning Chaos" of the new character, "Albions Emanation," is required to impose causality as a principle that determines narrative itself. However, the bid for determinacy made at the beginning of these lines is compromised by their conclusion. At the precise moment that a "cause" is being advanced, it is obscured. To what does "this" refer—the "way of the Devouring Power" or "Albions Emanation which he had hidden in Jealousy"? Does the second line mean that Albion's Emanation has been hidden by Albion as a consequence of his jealousy, or that it has been hidden and appears now in jealousy? Does "in Jealousy" function zeugmatically? And what are we to make of the apparent redundancy of "appearance in the frowning Chaos / . . . Appeard now in the frowning Chaos"? Is the temporal shift significant? Is Albions Emanation what appears in both cases, or is the intermediate line in which the words *Albions Emanation* appear also a zeugma? Is "Albions Emanation" a cause or an effect of an appearance? Or, and this is a reading that accords with the narrative voice's previous strategies, is the appearance of the signifier "Albions Emanation" (between this curious doubling of a completed act of appearing in a frowning Chaos followed by a present act of appearing in a frowning Chaos) a mirroring at the text's formal level of the actions described—a mirroring that is itself mirrored in the last line "Reflecting back to Albion"? (The absence of the apostrophe in "Albions Emanation" underdetermines reading Albion as plural or Albion as possessive.) This metamirroring, then, produces greater ambiguity about causality, chronology, and agency, precisely the ambiguity these lines seem to have been designed to stabilize: it is "prolific upon the Chaos."

The narrative voice assumes that the characters have a continuous and prior existence to the time they appear in the plate, and it also assumes that narrative has a referential function, presupposing and dependent upon a prior world/event/identity that it "simply" represents. The text deconstructs the self-justifying logic at work in the narrative voice's assertion of these priorities: the voice's legitimacy appears only as a function of the creation of the fiction of a prior state of affairs—of causality itself—and of the deliberate disguising of its fictional status. The "authority" of the voice requires that "causes," which are in fact a product of the activity of the authoritative voice, appear to predate the narrative; hence, the text's disclosure of a doubled chronology and self-divided *something*, here called "Albions Emanation," that is both cause and effect, an indication of the complex circular reasoning that must be instituted and then repressed in order to establish both a central authority and an ontologically prior spatiotemporal reality, a process of exclusion re-enacted by the editor who placed a period after the first mention of the frowning Chaos.

This passage reveals that causality is illegitimately invoked as the grounding for narratives that are strategically produced to stabilize identity and ratify authority. Significantly, this is the passage that first mentions the "Emanation" precisely at the moment when the narrative voice must project—as though describing an autonomous, precedent situation—the products of its own activities as independent of itself. What is being hidden/revealed in this passage about hiding/revelation is the voice's production of the Emanation as a necessary element underwriting its own authority.

The subversion of determinate causality and referential narrativity is tied to the subversion of essentialist or universalist notions of the self. "Albions Emanation" exists as a potentially separate entity within "Hermaphroditic / Albion," just as from various perspectives the Spectre, Albion, and the Divine Vision merge and separate. The attempts to stabilize these indeterminacies by narrative grounding or appeals to essentialized (gendered) identities depend upon the production of (apparently) exclusionary binary oppositions implicitly or explicitly hierarchized by reference to a transcendent subject: Divine Vision/Spectrous Chaos; Spectrous Chaos/Albion; Spectre (Satan)/God; Albion/Emanation; and finally Vala/Jerusalem. Crucial to the production of the binaries—and their function as markers of distinct identity—is a metaphysical appeal to a preceding history or reality within which these newly created characters are presumed to have existed, the prior causal ground that guarantees their existence. These binaries appear exclusively oppositional and capable of elucidating the coherence of personal identity insofar as they gain their legitimacy from the (disguised) fabrication of transcendental categories such as time and space, categories that are called into play to eradicate the vexing epistemology of causal relations. Without these categories to serve as reference points for causality, affirmations of the continuity of personal identity lose their force, as do "universally valid" claims about human nature, moral law, and so forth. Philosophical convictions (such as Kant's) about the transcendental status of subjectivity ultimately derive from a belief in the ontological priority and universality—the stability—of these categories. But if time and space themselves are functions of or products of the limited perceptions of a centralized subject, then, as Blake says at the conclusion of *Jerusalem*, in "creating exemplars of Memory and of Intellect / Creating Space, Creating Time," subjects produce "variation of Time & Space / Which vary according as the Organs of Perception vary" (Plate 98), a forceful return to the radically skeptical version of Hume's deconstruction of the self.

Associationist psychology presumes that the causal narrative of identity, constructed by an "experiential" memory, is the only possible narrative. Each new experience is linked to the next by spatiotemporal contiguity, and that relationship is fixed. On a skeptical analysis, this narratival account must be challenged from two fronts. First, if the contents of memory do not necessarily correspond to actual experience, if what we remember as the connection between experiences is a post hoc construction, then any number of narratives may be possible over the course of a lifetime, and any number may be operating at the same time. Furthermore, there is no necessary connection between the narrative of my identity that I "remember" at one time and the narrative of my identity that I "remember" at another if memory itself is faulty and subject to reconstruction.

In Plate 29/33, the Emanation who appears as an attempt to stabilize narrative proliferation is named "Vala": her appearance is "caused" only at the level of enunciation itself, in order to provide a post hoc illusion of an a priori ontological state of existence. In response to Albion's astonishment at her sudden and apparently *uncaused* appearance, Vala tries to make a case for the "reality" of the personal history she narrates. Her narration is designed to downplay Albion's discovery that she actually *has* appeared out of nowhere. She asserts her prior existence by narrating her history—the first personal history in the plate, which moves increasingly to expose as illusory the foundational claims of narrativity itself:

> I was a City & a Temple built by Albions Children.
> I was a Garden planted with beauty I allured on hill & valley
> The River of Life to flow against my walls & among my trees

Blake's Antimetaphysics and the Subject of Discourse

> Vala was Albions Bride & Wife in great Eternity
> The loveliest of the daughters of Eternity when in day-break.
> I emanated from Luvah over the Towers of Jerusalem
> And in her Courts among her little Children offering up
> The Sacrifice of fanatic love? why loved I Jerusalem:
> Why was I one with her embracing in the Vision of Jesus
> Wherefore did I loving create love. which never yet
> Immingled God & Man. when thou & I. hid the Divine Vision
> In cloud of secret gloom which behold involve me round about

Vala's contention that she existed prior to the moment of her emergence at the textual level of the plate—rather than being called into existence by the need to counteract indeterminate causality—enacts the metaphysical claims of narrativity. (The word *Vala* occurs earlier in the poem, of course, but not as the source of its own creation story.) But just as the previous sections of the plate have been unraveling the recursive logic of those narrative claims, so Vala's speech undermines her own ontological claims as well as those of other voices in the plate. Is Vala Albion's Emanation or Luvah's? If Vala was a "Temple built by Albions Children" and she was "Albions Bride & Wife," isn't the causal logic confused, a confusion echoed in "wherefore did I loving create love, which never yet"? Vala has no claim to be more "right" than any other voice/figure, but neither is she necessarily wrong. The identities and temporal relations cannot be straightened out by referring one part of the plate (or the poem) to another part, because all are implicated in the processes of narrative exclusion and repression that generate Vala and her speech.

Although it pretends to be so, Vala's history is not monolithic, teleological, or uncontested. Vala's self-contradictory narrative emerges as a stitching together of various incommensurate narrative possibilities: is Vala the primordial scene of biblical temptation or the product of the labors of the race of Cain? Contrary to the "story" in the narrative voice's passages, Vala "remembers" that she and Albion "hid the Divine Vision / In cloud of secret gloom." These conflictual stories not only problematize the transcendental status of any signifier, but they also suggest that all of the voices may be referring to the same events—the processes of generating coherence in the face of metaphysical uncertainty, or rather, in the face of the intertextual or dialogical state of affairs that is history/self/text/

world, a dialogical state that these characters prefer to understand as "Chaos" or to repress rather than to acknowledge.

The repression of discursive contestations is also thematized in the poem. Albion's reaction in the subsequent Plate 30/34 to the appearance of a narratival structure-as-character (Vala) who asserts an ontological priority ("Know me now Albion . . . I alone am Beauty / The Imaginative Human Form is but a breathing of Vala . . . from my secret Cave / Born of Woman") indicates the illegitimacy of such claims of precedence. In this next plate, Albion now "recognizes" Vala as "Nature." In other words, Albion "correctly" identifies the text's move to presume a reality to which it refers, a "material" world that is in fact a product of narrative processes that repress the dialogical or intertextual composition of the world. By acquiescing to the alleged ontological status of "nature," Albion becomes enthralled to this monoperspectival, "linguistic" materialism: "At thy word & at thy look death enrobes me about." In his acceptance of Vala's claims, Albion also reproduces the eighteenth-century dream of the adequation of the order of words to the order of things, hypothesizing that language can represent nature and that Nature—as so represented—is real. In this move, we see that Blake's delegitimation of metaphysical certainty extends to every topos—God, rationality, memory, tradition, identity, natural law, Nature—visited by eighteenth-century moral and political philosophy in its attempts to counter its own skeptical implications.[35]

---

35. See Isaac Kramnick's "Skepticism" for a discussion of the historicizing impulses of various skeptical positions in eighteenth-century political philosophy. See as well Nicholas Capaldi's *Hume's Place in Moral Philosophy* and Donald Livingston's *Hume's Philosophy of the Common Life* for the position that Hume understood the ideological constitution of society and subject. I agree with Capaldi and Livingston that the basis for such a conclusion appears in Hume's writings (I have already quoted one important reference to custom), but Hume himself consistently rejected the implications of his own analysis in favor of an appeal to universal human nature.

"The Dim Chaos Brightend" and a Possible Politics of Textuality

*I*n *Jerusalem*, the metaphysical moments—the conjuring of "reality," "identity," "truth," and so forth—that constitute ontological reality and the self-identical, continuous subject emerge as narrative constructs. Each achieves a temporary transcendental status that disappears when other conflicting or incommensurate narratives expose the exclusions enabling its fictitious transcendence. The limits to any given narrative's metaphysical claims cannot be discerned without an ideology of reading that both recapitulates conventional narrative assumptions (about causality, closure, referentiality, and so forth) and relies on a construction of the reader as a centralized, coherent subjectivity.

In this respect, Blake differs from his poststructuralist critics for whom "textuality" carries an ultimate value or serves as a telos to be realized. Blake's poem can be described by reference to "textuality," but in Blake this textuality is an idealization with a double valence. On the one hand, as a horizon of plurality ("liberty"), it can serve to authorize excursions from a trajectory of totalization; on the other hand, it can also emerge as the "spectre" of irrationality, disorder, and incomprehensibility ("Chaos"), the fear of which helps maintain the hegemony of totalization. Both representations are false: the horizon of free play can never be realized as such but can only appear as a function of the inevitably incomplete totalization of any system. Poststructuralist critics who seek to read Blake's poem as "liberatory" must work hard to repress the intuition that the horizon of an absolute textuality can only be realized through processes of determinacy.

It is a significant irony that a seminal description of "textuality"—Roland Barthes's own exposition in *S/Z*—also invokes and then suppresses this (Blakean) insight into the falsity of representing "textuality" as a realizable ideal. Barthes's description of textuality oscillates between the promotion of the desirability of realizing the plural text—"textuality" as such—and the recognition that "textuality" only comes into view for a determinate subject who attempts to impose determinate meaning:

> The writerly text is a perpetual present, upon which no *consequent* language (which would inevitably make it past) can be superimposed; the writerly text is *ourselves writing*, before the infinite play of the world (the world as function) is traversed, intersected, stopped, plasticized by some singular system (Ideology, Genus, Criticism) which reduces the plurality of entrances, the opening of networks, the infinity of many languages. . . . In this ideal text, the networks are many and interact, without any one of them being able to surpass the rest; this text is a galaxy of signifiers, not a structure of signifieds; it has no beginning, it is reversible; we gain access to it by several entrances, none of which can be authoritatively declared to be the main one; the codes it mobilizes extend *as far as the eye can reach*, they are indeterminable (meaning here is never subject to a principle of determination, unless by throwing dice). . . . All of which comes down to saying that for the plural text, there cannot be a narrative structure, a grammar, or a logic.[36]

Even though meaning is "never subject to determination," it is always narratival: "To read is to find meanings, and to find meanings is to name them; but these named meanings are swept toward other names; names call to each other, reassemble, and their grouping calls for further naming." However approximate, however indeterminate or endless, the "naming" of meaning always has a narratival structure, as recapitulated in Barthes's own "I pass, I intersect, I articulate, I release," the familiar narrative of romance. Of course, as Barthes describes it, the ideal plural text may not have a narratival structure, but we only glimpse the possibility of the writerly text by forging narratives, not by gaining access to a perception of "pure nonnarrativity." The plural text exists nowhere except as a plurality of narratives enacted through the process of reading, each of which seeks to repress other narratives *as* mere excess, chaos, or negligibility.

The apparent binary exclusions writerly/readerly, narrative/nonnarrative, system/nonsystem at work in Barthes's formulation cannot be maintained. "In operational terms, the meanings I find are

---

36. *S/Z*, 5–6. The subsequent quotes are from 11.

established not by "me" or by others, but by their *systematic* mark: there is no other *proof* of reading than the quality and endurance of its systematics." Narrativity *is* systematicity, an operation that constantly gestures toward fulfillment, determinacy, and metaphysics, but that always has to assert its own processes in the face of their failure. In fact, that failure is precisely what produces the impetus to narrate in the first place. Systematicity has a mark, narrative has a plot, because it does not occupy the entire field in which it moves. The "mark" of systematicity is its acknowledgment of its inability to totalize. If it were total, it would disappear from view. Nonetheless, this is not to say that what occupies the rest of the field is somehow nonnarratival, completely chaotic, unsystematic. The nonsystematic, the chaotic, the nonnarratival are equally invisible: when the specter of chaos is brought into play, it signifies the need for operations of exclusion and repression necessary to reduce to singularity (or weak plurality) a dialogically constituted field. Narrative does not order some primordial disorder, the "opposite" of narrative: narrative is all the world we have. We never see the "infinitude" of indeterminacy of the codes out of which our narratives take shape, because the horizon of plural codes only becomes perceivable (that is, only comes into being *for us*) by means of a process in which the reading subject enacts itself and the text narratively.

Implicit within Blake's text, then, as well as in Barthes's formulations, is a reading subject who discovers its own intertextual constitution processually, by performing what is essentially the Blakean Urizenic role of oppressor, limiter, excluder, divider, monologist, egotist, creator of order. This, I think, is not the direction in which Barthes wishes to go. For Barthes, the reader who reads in "scriptible" fashion acts in a partly free, partly bound way: free because the reader of a plural text asserts "the irresponsibility of the text" by "forgetting meanings"; bound because such a reader is already constructed by a "plurality of other texts." Barthes makes much less of the boundedness of the reader than of its freedom, whereas I maintain that inherent in the "forgetting" is a repression of competing meaning, a repression enacted precisely to limit the text to an apparently determinate and final meaning. The process of this forgetting, repression, exclusion, and privileging results in a performance of a plural text, but the plurality is formed out of narratives designed to limit. The reading subject who obsessively establishes order by attending to signs of "disorder" (signs that any given system or ordering fails to account for the entire field, signs of excess) must just as obsessively deconstruct its own systems in order to construct new, more "inclusive" ones. This task is never-ending; it is a frenetic and ultimately inadequate activity designed to fend off the "threat" of "Chaos" or plurality and mounted by the centralized subject armed with a metaphysics of order that can only wearisomely reproduce the very threat against which it strives. The value of textuality as an ideal, then, inheres in its potential to disrupt *momentarily* a given process of ordering so that another can take its place. That is to say, at any given moment, some signifying networks are privileged over others, but that privilege is not absolute. Both the construction and the deconstruction are crucial, but the deconstructive moments do not represent an "escape" from the continual construction of horizons of limitation on which our agency depends. Barthes's recurrent use of visual metaphors ("as far as the eye can see," "horizon," "image") underscores the importance of the activity of this subject, who creates a "horizon" out of its phenomenal centrality, its "Selfhood." Its search for mastery is a narrative of "errors": this is the "story" of *Jerusalem*. At any moment in the search, the reading subject can acknowledge the structure of what it has produced, a structure that articulates disjunct, incommensurable, or competing systems as though they derive from a transcendental subject and form a coherent totality. The constructed nature of the "ontologically real" or the "metaphysically true" or the "self-identical person"—and the illegitimate forms of authority that these notions ratify—comes into view only by means of a reliance on precisely those "transcendental" positions, the limitations of which appear only when they are mobilized. The "errors" mark the points of competition, excess, and inadequacy of all totalizing gestures, just as they form the only means for understanding that inadequacy.

A Bakhtinian understanding of dialogism, on the other hand, already takes into account the importance of the limitation and contestation of utterances and discourses. As Todorov writes:

> If we go now . . . to the set of utterances that constitute the verbal life of the community, one fact appears, to Bakhtin, more striking

than all others: the existence of *types* of utterances, or discourses, in a relatively high but nonetheless limited number. Two excesses are to be avoided here: to recognize only the diversity of languages and ignore that of utterances; to imagine that this last variety is individual and therefore unlimited. The stress is not on the plurality but on the difference . . . To name this irreducible diversity of discursive types, Bakhtin introduces a neologism, raznorecie . . . *heterology*.[37]

In noting Bakhtin's insistence that no utterance or discourse exists independently of a relationship to other utterances or discourses, a relationship denominated as "dialogical" or "intertextual," Todorov also remarks that there is a countertendency in Bakhtin to reestablish a binary opposition between intertextuality and its absence, or between dialogism and "monologism."[38] Monologism is the dream of positivistic science and the deluded speech of the possessive Selfhood.

This discussion suggests that Blake's analysis has a political resonance that speaks to the charges of depoliticization leveled against deconstructive versions of poststructuralism. Obviously, Blake's text is not a treatise of political or moral philosophy. And even if it implicitly invokes some concept of repression, the Blakean exposition of an intertextual subjectivity does not constitute a psychology.[39] It is equally obvious that the text concerns itself fundamentally with issues of individuality, even though its dialogism and its conclusion point to Blake's understanding of the sociality of the subjectivity. To go further, the Blakean subject is in some sense congenial to a humanist position—and a potentially reactionary one at that—insofar as all political change is situated at the level of individual consciousness and capacity for self-transformation.

However, once the individual is understood as an epiphenome-

37. *Mikhail Bakhtin: The Dialogical Principle*, 56.
38. Ibid., 60ff.
39. I make this comment in part in response to Damrosch's claims that the Blakean self has no unconscious. My understanding of Blake's analysis of subjectivity includes the subject's potential lack of awareness of the forces constituting it and the lack of awareness of this lack of awareness. Damrosch often seems to read the speeches by Los, the Spectre, and Albion as if we can take the degree of their self-knowledge to represent everything that Blake would have us learn from them.

non of a limited intertextuality—the limitations of which are historically and locally specified—then the Blakean text provides tools of ideological analysis, even if it does not offer a political program.[40] Depending upon whether the reader considers such ideological analysis itself to be a precondition for political change, he or she will evaluate the Blakean text as potentially revolutionary or as irrelevant for praxis. Blake never claims that the identification of the limits of contraction or the ideologies of oppression or the enabling tropes of authority will liberate humankind from history or elevate it to universal or transcendental status. But it may help to find local points of resistance to the forms of hegemony in which all subjects are implicated.

The foregoing remarks could serve to remind us that in all political philosophy (and in economic theory as well) some theorizing of the mediation between individual subjects and larger social structures must take place, overtly or covertly. In the majority of liberal political philosophy, that mediation is accomplished by recourse to universalizing notions of human nature.[41] In the case of traditional Marxism, the point of mediation is the ideological construction of consciousness, itself mediated by those larger structures (even though, of course, Marx too relies on a universal human nature). Those poststructuralist literary theories that take their start from a criticism of the apparent depoliticization of deconstructive strategies and that seek a political understanding of the relations between cultural practices, institutions, and individual behavior have most recently acknowledged the inadequacy of their own conceptions of that mediation point, focusing in particular on the need for a theory of

---

40. I have thought that one productive intertextual reading of *Jerusalem* would consider the interactions of the characters as unfolding the drama of the issues, problems, and criticisms of the Hobbesian analysis of the genesis of government, if the additional stipulation that the Hobbesian individual in a state of war is a prediscursive entity is applied. Then the intertextual dimension of the characters would emerge as functions of ideology; at the same time we would see the emergence of a contestatory discursive field. The Hobbesian sovereign would represent the monological determinism of an appeal to "divine" signifiers, for example, in the Blakean text.

41. For example, John Rawls's seminal *A Theory of Justice* presupposes a human nature that Rawls himself comes to admit is simply a representation of American Puritan ideology.

the historically differentiated *reception* and processing of cultural phenomena.[42]

Blake's poem constantly reemphasizes the importance of the partiality (in both senses of particularity and limitation) of subjectivity, the situatedness of the audience of any given speech, the variability of perspective that can be taken on any given event, the role of ideology in shaping consciousness, and the nonlinear forms of determinacy that inevitably come into play when these heterogeneous, heterological, and heterontological forces intersect. Donna Haraway theorizes the political relevance of partial subjectivity:

> *All* components of the desire [for recognizing our own "semiotic technologies" for making meanings, the radical historical contingency for all knowledge claims and knowing subjects, and the need for accounts of a "real" world that can be partially shared] are paradoxical and dangerous, and their combination is both contradictory and necessary. Feminists don't need a doctrine of objectivity that promises transcendence, a story that loses track of its mediations just where someone might be held responsible for something, and unlimited instrumental power. We don't want a theory of innocent powers to represent the world, where language and bodies both fall into the bliss of organic symbiosis. We also don't want to theorize the world, much less act within it, in terms of Global Systems, but we do need an earthwide network of connections, including the ability partially to translate knowledges among very different—and power-differentiated—communities. We need the power of modern critical theories of how meanings get made, not in order to deny meanings and bodies, but in order to build meanings and bodies that have a chance for life.[43]

The enactment of the textuality of *Jerusalem* can bring its readers to an experience of this partiality and situatedness, of the desire and drive for determinacy and its contradictory effects, a Vala/Jerusalem desire that is eternally double.

---

42. Several articles in cultural studies and multicultural feminism in particular have outlined such a need, the importance of which can easily be demonstrated when we realize the extent to which essentialism and universalization have determined the so-called "findings" of cultural criticism. See, for example, the series of essays collected in *Differences: A Journal of Feminist Cultural Studies* 1.2, entitled *The Essential Difference: Another Look at Essentialism* (Summer 1989).

43. "Situated Knowledges: The Science Question in Feminism and the Privilege of Partial Perspective," 579–80.

With these caveats in mind, let me return to some lines from the close of *Jerusalem*: "the dim Chaos brightend beneath. above, around: Eyed as the Peacock / According to the Nerves of Human Sensation." These lines suggest several competing interpretations. One interpretation I have suggested in the Introduction construes these lines to mean that the obscure chaos of meaninglessness at the horizon of the centralized subject can regain its potential meaningfulness by recourse to the displacement of the centralized subject. On the other hand, the critique of subjectivity-as-coherence in the Blakean text may give rise to the conception of a universe that is entirely—and infinitely—intertextual. On such a view, the "dim Chaos" would refer to the idealized version of "textuality," the ahistorical and transcendent version of textuality we find in Barthes's text, while the "brightening" of that chaos would not in any sense monologically determine a structure or meaning but would instead make it visible in its historical specificity, its relationship to particular subject positions. But other possibilities present themselves. What does it mean to be "Eyed as the Peacock"? In the two previous sections I have taken this to mean figuratively that numerous phenomenalistic subject positions or historical subject positions have to come into play. But the phenomenal peacock has only two eyes, and its traditional signification refers to the vainglorious ego ("I-ed"?). Hence, the lines also suggest that the brightening of chaos requires the centralized subject as a precondition for meaningfulness. The implications of this reading are underscored by the recognition that the eyes on the peacock's tail are not seeing eyes. If they were, we could take indefinite multiple perspectives; but since they are not, they may refer both to the limit of contraction of the "nerves of sensation" of the centralized subject and—the darkest reading—to the limitation on our identificatory capabilities to those forms that are already in some sense given to us.

From one perspective this last conclusion is disheartening: it seems to say that no matter how much effort we put into recognizing our own participation in oppression, or into cognizing the mechanisms and structures of ideological construction, we never escape. Yet, another view says that if ideological or narratival contestations are all the world and all we have, then they are our best tools for creating better (if not optimal) conditions for ourselves. What is more, the continual reinscription of the limitation of subjectivity for transcending its historical conditions is in itself a barrier to making the kinds of metaphysical gestures, exclusions, negations, oppositions, and hierarchies that ground "unassailable" authority. And finally, the "chaos" that we find here may help "undetermine" the effects of any given ideology, standing as a signifier of the competing, contestatory ideological field that both calls for determinate stabilizing gestures and inevitably produces a variety of claims to legitimacy of its incommensurable "system." If "reality" is intertextual (conflictual, differential, multi-ideological), then there can be no space of utter disorder any more than there can be a space of utter determinacy.[44] Attempts to impose monologism—as well as absolute boundaries between oppositions—will reveal/produce "intertextuality" if we attend to the excesses and supplements such attempts seek to repress. The Blakean lines are not apocalyptic: not much changes—a dim Chaos gets somewhat brighter—but at least we come to understand how tyranny arises in Paradise as well as in Pandemonium.

---

44. Many readers will recognize one of the principles of chaos theory at work here. Those interested might look at N. Katherine Hayles's collection of essays entitled *Chaos and Order*.

Bibliography

Ackland, Michael. "Blake's Critique of Enlightenment Reason in *The Four Zoas*." *Colby Library Quarterly* 19 (September 1983): 173–89.
Adams, Hazard. "Blake, *Jerusalem*, and Symbolic Form." *Blake Studies* 7 (1975): 143–66.
———. "Blake and the Postmodern." In *William Blake: Essays for S. Foster Damon*, edited by Alvin H. Rosenfeld, 3–17. Providence, R.I.: Brown University Press, 1969.
———. "Must a Poem Be a Perfect Unity?" *Blake/An Illustrated Quarterly* 21 (Fall 1987): 74–77.
———. *Philosophy of the Literary Symbolic*. Tallahassee: University Presses of Florida, 1983.
———. "Post-Essick Prophecy." *Studies in Romanticism* 21 (Fall 1982): 400–403.
———. "Synecdoche and Method." In *Blake and the Argument of Method*, edited by Dan Miller, Mark Bracher, and Donald Ault, 41–71. Durham and London: Duke University Press, 1987.
———. *William Blake: A Reading of the Shorter Poems*. Seattle: University of Washington Press, 1963.
Althusser, Louis. "Ideology and Ideological State Apparatuses." In *Lenin and Philosophy and Other Essays*, translated by Ben Brewster, 121–73. New York: Monthly Review Press, 1971.
Altizer, Thomas J. *The New Apocalypse: The Radical Christian Vision of William Blake*. East Lansing: Michigan State University Press, 1967.
Anderson, Mark. "Why Is That Fairy in *Europe*?" *Colby Library Quarterly* 21 (September 1985): 122–33.
Augustine. *The Confessions of Saint Augustine*. Translated by Edward B. Pusey, D.D. New York: Random House, 1949.
———. *On Christian Doctrine*. Translated by D. W. Robertson, Jr. New York: Library of Liberal Arts, 1958.

Ault, Donald. *Narrative Unbound: Re-Visioning William Blake's "The Four Zoas."* Barrytown, N.Y.: Station Hill Press, 1987.

———. "Re-Visioning *The Four Zoas*." In *Unnam'd Forms: Blake and Textuality*, edited by Nelson Hilton and Thomas A. Vogler, 105–39. Berkeley: University of California Press, 1986.

Barthes, Roland. "From Work to Text." In *Textual Strategies: Perspectives in Post-Structuralist Criticism*, edited by Josué V. Harari, 72–81. Ithaca: Cornell University Press, 1979.

———. *S/Z*. Translated by Richard Miller. New York: Hill and Wang, 1974.

Beer, John. *Blake's Humanism*. Manchester: University of Manchester Press, 1968.

Behrendt, Stephen C. " 'The Consequence of High Powers': Blake, Shelley, and Prophecy's Public Dimension." *Papers on Language and Literature* 22 (Summer 1986): 254–75.

———. " 'This Accursed Family': Blake's *America* and the American Revolution." *The Eighteenth Century: Theory and Interpretation* 27 (1986): 26–51.

Bender, John, and Anne Mellor. "Liberating the Sister Arts: The Revolution of Blake's 'Infant Sorrow.'" *English Literary History* 50 (1983): 297–319.

Bentley, Gerald E., Jr. "Blake and the Antients: A Prophet with Honour among the Sons of God." *The Huntington Library Quarterly* (Winter 1983): 1–17.

———. *Blake Records*. Oxford: The Clarendon Press, 1969.

———. *Blake Records Supplement*. Oxford: The Clarendon Press, 1988.

———. "Blake's Techniques of Engraving and Printing." *Studies in Bibliography* 34: 241–53.

Berninghausen, Thomas. "The Marriage of Two Contraries in 'To Tirzah.'" *Colby Library Quarterly* 20 (December 1984): 191–98.

Berry, Boyd. *Process of Speech: Puritan Religious Writing and "Paradise Lost."* Baltimore: The Johns Hopkins University Press, 1976.

Bertholf, Robert J., and Annette S. Levitt, eds. *Blake and the Moderns*. Albany: State University of New York Press, 1982.

Billigheimer, Rachel. "Blake's 'Eyes of God': Cycles to Apocalypse and Redemption." *Philological Quarterly* 66 (Spring 1987): 231–58.

———. "The Eighth Eye: Prophetic Vision in Blake's Poetry and Design." *Colby Library Quarterly* 22 (June 1986): 93–110.

Bindman, David. "Blake's Theory and Practice of Imitation." In *Blake in His Time*, edited by Robert N. Essick and Donald Pearce, 91–98. Bloomington: Indiana University Press, 1978.

Blake, William. *The Complete Poetry and Prose of William Blake*. Edited by David V. Erdman. Berkeley: University of California Press, 1982.

———. *Jerusalem*. New York: The Beechhurst Press, 1955.

Bloom, Harold. *The Anxiety of Influence: A Theory of Poetry*. Oxford: Oxford University Press, 1973.

———. "Blake's *Jerusalem*: The Bard of Sensibility and the Form of Prophecy." *Eighteenth-Century Studies* 4 (1970): 6–20.

———. "Commentary." In *The Complete Poetry and Prose of William Blake*, edited by David V. Erdman, 894–970. Berkeley: University of California Press, 1982.

———. "Dialectic in *The Marriage of Heaven and Hell*." *PMLA* 83 (December 1958): 501–4.

———, ed. *William Blake's "The Marriage of Heaven and Hell."* New York: Chelsea House Publishers, 1987.

Blunt, Anthony. *The Art of William Blake*. New York: Columbia University Press, 1959.

Bogan, James. "Blake's City of Golgonooza in *Jerusalem*: Metaphor and Mandala." *Colby Library Quarterly* 17 (June 1981): 85–98.

Bracher, Mark. "The Metaphysical Grounds of Oppression in Blake's *Visions of the Daughters of Albion*." *Colby Library Quarterly* 20 (September 1984): 164–75.

Bratton, Fred Gladstone. *A History of the Bible: An Introduction to the Historical Method*. Boston: Beacon Press, 1967.

Brenkman, John. "A Poetics of Moral Revaluation: 'A Poison Tree.'" In *Culture and Domination*, 111–21. Ithaca and London: Cornell University Press, 1985.

———. "Poetry and Politics: 'London.'" In *Culture and Domination*, 121–38. Ithaca and London: Cornell University Press, 1985.

Brinkley, Robert A. "Blake and the Prophecy of Satan." *The New Orleans Review* (Fall 1982): 73–76.

Brisman, Leslie. "Re: Generation in Blake." *Romantic Origins*. Ithaca and London: Cornell University Press, 1978.

Brumm, Ursula. *American Thought and Religious Typology*. Translated by John Hoaglund. New Brunswick: Rutgers University Press, 1970.

Burke, Kenneth. *A Grammar of Motives*. Berkeley: University of California Press, 1945.

Butler, Marilyn. *Romantics, Rebels, and Reactionaries: English Literature and Its Background, 1760–1830*. Oxford: Oxford University Press, 1981.

Capaldi, Nicholas. *Hume's Place in Moral Philosophy*. New York: Peter Lang Publishing, 1987.

Carr, Stephen Leo. "Illuminated Printing: Toward a Logic of Difference." In *Unnam'd Forms: Blake and Textuality*, edited by Nelson Hilton and Thomas A. Vogler, 177–96. Berkeley: University of California Press, 1986.

———. "Visionary Syntax: Nontyrannical Coherence in Blake's Visual Art." *The Eighteenth Century: Theory and Interpretation* 22 (1981): 222–48.

Carroll, David. *The Subject in Question: The Languages of Theory and the Strategies of Fiction*. Chicago: The University of Chicago Press, 1982.

Chayes, Irene H. "Blake's Ways with Art Sources: Michelangelo's *The Last Judgment*." *Colby Library Quarterly* 20 (June 1984): 60–89.

Coleridge, Samuel Taylor. *Selected Poetry and Prose*. Edited by Donald A. Stauffer. New York: Random House, 1951.

Compagnon, Antoine. *La seconde main ou le travail de la citation*. Paris: Éditions du Seuil, 1979.

Cooper, Andrew. "Blake's Escape from Mythology: Self-Mastery in *Milton*." *Studies in Romanticism* 20 (Spring 1981): 85–110.

Copleston, Frederick. *A History of Philosophy*. Book 2, vol. 5, *Seventeenth- and Eighteenth-Century British Philosophers*. New York: Doubleday, 1985.

Corlett, William S. "Pocock, Foucault, Forces of Reassurance." *Political Theory* 17 (February 1989): 77–100.

Cowper, William. "The Task." In *Complete Poetical Works of William Cowper, Esq*. New York: Appleton, 1869.

Curran, Stuart. *Poetic Form and British Romanticism*. New York and Oxford: Oxford University Press, 1986.

———. "The Structures of *Jerusalem*." In *Blake's Sublime Allegory*, edited by Stuart Curran and Joseph Anthony Wittreich, Jr., 329–46. Madison: University of Wisconsin Press, 1973.

Curran, Stuart, and Joseph Anthony Wittreich, Jr., eds. *Blake's Sublime Allegory*. Madison: University of Wisconsin Press, 1973.

Damrosch, Leopold, Jr. "Burns, Blake, and the Recovery of Lyric." *Studies in Romanticism* 21 (Winter 1982): 637–60.
———. *Symbol and Truth in Blake's Myth*. Princeton: Princeton University Press, 1980.
Davis, Patricia Elizabeth. "Revelation in Blake's *Job.*" *Philological Quarterly* 65 (Fall 1986): 447–78.
Deleuze, Gilles. *Kant's Critical Philosophy*. Translated by Hugh Tomlinson and Barbara Habberjam. Minneapolis: University of Minnesota Press, 1984.
De Luca, Vincent. "Blake and the Two Sublimes." In *Studies in Eighteenth-Century Culture* 11, edited by Harry C. Payne, 93–105. Madison: University of Wisconsin Press, 1982.
———. "A Wall of Words: The Sublime as Text." In *Unnam'd Forms: Blake and Textuality*, edited by Nelson Hilton and Thomas A. Vogler, 218–41. Berkeley: University of California Press, 1986.
De Man, Paul. *Blindness and Insight: Essays in the Rhetoric of Contemporary Criticism*. 2d rev. ed. Minneapolis: University of Minnesota Press, 1983.
Derrida, Jacques. *Of Grammatology*. Translated by Gayatry Chakravorty Spivak. Baltimore: Johns Hopkins University Press, 1974.
———. "Signature Event Context." In *Margins of Philosophy*, translated by Alan Bass, 307–30. Chicago: The University of Chicago Press, 1982.
———. *Speech and Phenomena*. Translated by David B. Allison. Evanston: Northwestern University Press, 1973.
Descombes, Vincent. *Modern French Philosophy*. Translated by L. Scott-Fox and J. M. Harding. Cambridge: Cambridge University Press, 1980.
———. "Subjectivity and Individuality." Draft manuscript.
De Sola Pinto, Vivian, ed. *The Divine Vision: Studies in the Poetry and Art of William Blake*. London: Victor Gollancz, 1957.
DiSalvo, Jackie. *War of Titans: Blake's Critique of Milton and the Politics of Religion*. Pittsburgh: University of Pittsburgh Press, 1983.
Doskow, Minna. "The Humanized Universe of Blake and Marx." In *Blake and the Moderns*, edited by Robert J. Bertholf and Annette S. Levitt, 225–40. Albany: State University of New York Press, 1982.
———. "The Shape of Limitation: A Visual Pattern in the Illuminated Works of William Blake." *Colby Library Quarterly* 17 (September 1981): 121–60.

Easson, Roger. "William Blake and His Reader in *Jerusalem*." In *Blake's Sublime Allegory*, edited by Stuart Curran and Joseph Anthony Wittreich, Jr., 309–28. Madison: University of Wisconsin Press, 1973.

Eaves, Morris. "Introduction to Inside the Blake Industry: Past, Present, and Future." *Studies in Romanticism* 21 (Fall 1982): 389–90.

———. *William Blake's Theory of Art*. Princeton: Princeton University Press, 1982.

Eaves, Morris, and Michael Fischer, eds. *Romanticism and Contemporary Criticism*. Ithaca and London: Cornell University Press, 1986.

Erdman, David V. *Blake: Prophet against Empire*. 3d ed. Princeton: Princeton University Press, 1977.

———. *The Illuminated Blake*. Garden City, N.Y.: Anchor Books, 1974.

———. "The Symmetries of *The Song of Los*." *Studies in Romanticism* 16 (Spring 1977): 179–88.

Erdman, David V., and John E. Grant, eds. *Blake's Visionary Forms Dramatic*. Princeton: Princeton University Press, 1970.

Essick, Robert. "*The Four Zoas*: Intention and Production." *Blake/An Illustrated Quarterly* 18 (Spring 1985): 216–20.

———. "How Blake's Body Means," In *Unnam'd Forms: Blake and Textuality*, edited by Nelson Hilton and Thomas A. Vogler, 197–217. Berkeley: University of California Press, 1986.

———. *William Blake, Printmaker*. Princeton: Princeton University Press, 1980.

———. "William Blake, William Hamilton, and the Materials of Graphic Meaning." *English Literary History* 52 (Winter 1985): 833–72.

Essick, Robert N., and Donald Pearce, eds. *Blake in His Time*. Bloomington: Indiana University Press, 1978.

Ferber, Michael. "London and Its Politics." *English Literary History* 48 (1981): 310–38.

Fischer, Michael. "William Blake's Quarrel with Indeterminacy." *The New Orleans Review* (Winter 1983): 43–49.

Fischer, Peter. "Blake's Attacks on the Classical Tradition." *Philological Quarterly* 50 (1961): 1–18.

Fish, Stanley. *Self-Consuming Artifacts*. Berkeley: University of California Press, 1972.

———. *Surprised by Sin*. Berkeley: University of California Press, 1971.

Fogel, Aaron. "Pictures of Speech: On Blake's Poetic." *Studies in Romanticism* 21 (Summer 1982): 217–42.
Folkenflik, Robert. "Macpherson, Chatterton, Blake and the Great Age of Literary Forgery." *Centennial Review* 18 (Fall 1974): 378–91.
Foucault, Michel. "What Is an Author?" In *Textual Strategies: Perspectives in Post-Structuralist Criticism*, edited by Josué V. Harari, 141–60. Ithaca: Cornell University Press, 1979.
Fox, Susan. *Poetic Form in Blake's "Milton."* Princeton: Princeton University Press, 1976.
Frei, Hans W. *The Eclipse of Biblical Narrative: A Study in Eighteenth- and Nineteenth-Century Hermeneutics*. New Haven and London: Yale University Press, 1974.
Frosch, Douglas. *The Awakening of Albion*. Ithaca and London: Cornell University Press, 1974.
Fruchtman, Jack, Jr. "Politics and the Apocalypse: The Republic and the Millenium in Late Eighteenth-Century English Political Thought." In *Studies in Eighteenth-Century Culture* 10, edited by Harry C. Payne, 153–64. Madison: University of Wisconsin Press, 1981.
Fry, Paul. *The Reach of Criticism*. New Haven and London: Yale University Press, 1983.
Frye, Northrop. *Fearful Symmetry*. Princeton: Princeton University Press, 1947.
———. *The Great Code: The Bible and Literature*. San Diego, New York, and London: Harcourt, Brace, Jovanovich, 1982.
———, ed. *Blake*. Englewood Cliffs, N.J.: Prentice-Hall, 1966.
Fuller, Reginald C. *Alexander Geddes: Pioneer of Biblical Criticism*. Sheffield: The Almond Press, 1984.
Gallagher, Philip J. "The Word Made Flesh: Blake's 'A Poison Tree' and the Book of Genesis." *Studies in Romanticism* 16 (Spring 1977): 237–49.
Geddes, Alexander. *Proposals for printing by a subscription a new translation of the Holy Bible, from corrected texts of the originals*. London: Joseph Johnson, 1788.
———. *Prospectus of a new translation of the Holy Bible*. London: R. Faulder, Bond Street, 1786.
Gleckner, Robert. "Antithetical Structure in Blake's 'Poetical Sketches.'" *Studies in Romanticism* 20 (Summer 1981): 143–61.

———. "Blake's 'Little Black Boy' and the Bible." *Colby Library Quarterly* 18 (December 1982): 205–13.

———. *The Piper and the Bard*. Detroit: Wayne State University Press, 1959.

Grant, John E., ed. *Discussion of William Blake*. Boston: D. C. Heath and Company, 1961.

Gray, Thomas. "The Bard." In *The Complete English Poems of Thomas Gray*, edited by James Reeves. New York: Harper and Row, 1973.

Greenberg, Mark L. "Blake's 'Science.'" In *Studies in Eighteenth-Century Culture* 12, edited by Harry C. Payne, 115–30. Madison: University of Wisconsin Press, 1983.

Gross, David. " 'Mind-Forg'd Manacles': Hegemony and Counter-Hegemony in Blake." *The Eighteenth Century: Theory and Interpretation* 27 (1986): 3–25.

Hagstrum, Jean. *William Blake: Poet and Painter*. Chicago: The University of Chicago Press, 1978.

Haraway, Donna. "Situated Knowledges: The Science Question in Feminism and the Privilege of Partial Perspective." *Feminist Studies* 14 (Fall 1988): 575–99.

Harris, Victor. "Allegory to Analogy in the Interpretation of Scriptures." *Philological Quarterly* 45 (1966): 1–23.

Hartman, Geoffrey. "Envoi: 'So Many Things.'" In *Unnam'd Forms: Blake and Textuality*, edited by Nelson Hilton and Thomas A. Vogler, 242–48. Berkeley: University of California Press, 1986.

———. "The Progress of Poesy." In *Beyond Formalism*, 193–205. New Haven and London: Yale University Press, 1970.

Hayles, N. Katherine. *Chaos Bound: Entropy, Information, and Complexity in Contemporary Literature and Science*. Ithaca: Cornell University Press, 1990.

———, ed. *Chaos and Order*. Chicago: University of Chicago Press, 1991.

Hill, Christopher. *The World Turned Upside Down: Radical Ideas during the English Revolution*. New York: Viking, 1972.

Hilton, Nelson. "Blakean Zen." *Studies in Romanticism* 24 (Summer 1985): 183–200.

———. *Literal Imagination: Blake's Vision of Words*. Berkeley: University of California Press, 1983.

———. "An Original Story." In *Unnam'd Forms: Blake and Textuality*, edited by Nelson Hilton and Thomas A. Vogler, 69–104. Berkeley: University of California Press, 1986.

———, ed. *Essential Articles for the Study of William Blake, 1970–1984*. Hamden, Conn.: The Shoe String Press, 1986.

Hilton, Nelson, and Thomas A. Vogler, eds. *Unnam'd Forms: Blake and Textuality*. Berkeley: University of California Press, 1986.

Hirsch, E. D. *Innocence and Experience: An Introduction to Blake*. New Haven: Yale University Press, 1964.

Hoagwood, Terence Allan. "Pictorial Apocalypse: Blake's 'Great Red Dragon and the Woman Clothed with the Sun.'" *Colby Library Quarterly* 21 (March 1985): 11–21.

———. *Prophecy and the Philosophy of Mind: Traditions of Blake and Shelley*. University, Al.: The University of Alabama Press, 1985.

Horn, William Dennis. "Blake and the Problematic of Self." In *Blake and the Moderns*, edited by Robert J. Bertholf and Annette S. Levitt, 260–85. Albany: State University of New York Press, 1982.

———. "Blake's Revisionism: Gnostic Interpretation and Critical Methodology." In *Blake and the Argument of Method*, edited by Dan Miller, Mark Bracher, and Donald Ault, 72–98. Durham and London: Duke University Press, 1987.

Howard, John. *Blake's Milton: A Study in the Selfhood*. Cranbury, N.J.: Associated University Presses, 1976.

———. *Infernal Poetics: Poetic Structures in Blake's Lambeth Prophecies*. Cranbury, N.J.: Associated University Presses, 1984.

Howes, Thomas. "Doubts Concerning the Translation and Notes of the Bishop of London to Isaiah, Vindicating Ezekiel, Isaiah, and other Jewish Prophets from Disorder in Arrangement." *Critical Observations on Books, Ancient and Modern*. Vol. 2, *1776–1813*. Cited in Leslie Tannenbaum, *Biblical Tradition in Blake's Early Prophecies: The Great Code of Art*. Princeton: Princeton University Press, 1982.

Hume, David. *Enquiry Concerning Human Understanding*. Edited by L. A. Selby-Bigge. Oxford: Oxford University Press, 1951.

———. *A Treatise of Human Nature*. Edited by L. A. Selby-Bigge. Oxford: Oxford University Press, 1951.

Husserl, Edmund. *Ideas: General Introduction to Pure Phenomenology*. Translated by W. R. Boyce Gibson. New York: Macmillan Publishing Company, 1931.

James, David E. "Blake's *Laocoon*: A Degree Zero of Literary Production." *PMLA* 98 (January 1983): 226–36.

———. *Written Within and Without: A Study of Blake's "Milton."* Frankfurt am Main: Verlag Peter Lang GmbH, 1977.

Kermode, Frank. *The Genesis of Secrecy: On the Interpretation of Narrative*. Cambridge and London: Harvard University Press, 1979.

Keynes, Geoffrey. *Blake Studies: Essays on His Life and Work*. Oxford: The Clarendon Press, 1971.

Kiralis, Karl. "The Theme and Structure of William Blake's *Jerusalem*." In *The Divine Vision: Studies in the Poetry and Art of William Blake*, edited by Vivian de Sola Pinto, 141–62. London: Victor Gollancz, 1957.

Korshin, Paul J. "The Development of Abstracted Typology in England, 1650–1820." In *Literary Uses of Typology*, edited by Earl Miner, 147–203. Princeton: Princeton University Press, 1977.

Kramnick, Isaac. "Skepticism in English Political Thought: From Temple to Burke." *Studies in Burke and His Time* 12 (Fall 1970): 1627–60.

Kroeber, Karl. "Delivering *Jerusalem*." In *Blake's Sublime Allegory*, edited by Stuart Curran and Joseph Anthony Wittreich, Jr., 347–67. Madison: University of Wisconsin Press, 1973.

Kroll, Richard. "Mise-en-Page, Biblical Criticism, and Inference during the Restoration." In *Studies in Eighteenth-Century Culture* 16, edited by O. M. Brack, Jr., 3–40. Madison: The University of Wisconsin Press, 1987.

Latane, David E., Jr. "The Door into *Jerusalem*." *Romanticism Past and Present* 7 (Summer 1983): 17–26.

Lee, Judith. "Ways of Their Own: The Emanations of Blake's *Vala, or The Four Zoas*." *English Literary History* 50 (Spring 1983): 131–53.

Lesnick, Harry. "Narrative Structure and the Antithetical Vision of *Jerusalem*." In *Blake's Visionary Forms Dramatic*, edited by David V. Erdman and John E. Grant, 391–412. Princeton: Princeton University Press, 1970.

Linkin, Harriet Kramer. "The Function of Dialogue in *The Book of Thel*." *Colby Library Quarterly* 23 (June 1987): 66–76.

Livingston, Donald. *Hume's Philosophy of the Common Life*. Chicago: University of Chicago Press, 1984.

Lowth, Robert. *Lectures on the Sacred Poetry of the Hebrews*. New York: Garland Publishing, 1971.

McCord, James. "Historical Dissonance and William Blake's *The Song of Los.*" *Colby Library Quarterly* 20 (March 1984): 22–35.
McGann, Jerome J. "The Aim of Blake's Prophecies and the Uses of Blake Criticism." In *Blake's Sublime Allegory*, edited by Stuart Curran and Joseph Anthony Wittreich, Jr., 3–22. Madison: University of Wisconsin Press, 1973.
———. "The Idea of an Indeterminate Text: Blake's Bible of Hell and Dr. Alexander Geddes." *Studies in Romanticism* 25 (Fall 1986): 303–24.
———. "The Meaning of the Ancient Mariner." *Critical Inquiry* (Autumn 1981): 34–67.
———. "The Text, the Poem, and the Problem of Historical Method." *New Literary History* 12 (Winter 1981) 269–88.
Madison, Gary Brent. *The Phenomenology of Merleau-Ponty*. Athens: Ohio University Press, 1981.
Mann, Paul. *"The Book of Urizen* and the Horizon of the Book." In *Unnam'd Forms: Blake and Textuality*, edited by Nelson Hilton and Thomas A. Vogler, 49–68. Berkeley: University of California Press, 1986.
———. "The Final State of *The Four Zoas.*" *Blake/An Illustrated Quarterly* (Spring 1985): 204–9.
Marin, Louis. *Détruire la peinture*. Paris: Éditions Galilée, 1977.
Marks, Mollyanne. "Renovation of Form: Time as Hero in Blake's Major Prophecies." In *Studies in Eighteenth-Century Culture* 5, edited by Ronald C. Rosbottom, 55–66. Madison: The University of Wisconsin Press, 1976.
Markus, R. A. "St. Augustine on Signs." In *Augustine*, edited by R. A. Markus, 61–91. New York: Doubleday and Company, 1972.
Martin, Richard G. "Material Differences: The Immaterialisms of Berkeley and Blake." *English Studies in Canada* 13 (December 1987): 391–405.
Mazzeo, J. A. *Renaissance and Eighteenth-Century Studies*. New York: Columbia University Press, 1964.
Mellor, Anne Kostelanetz. *Blake's Human Form Divine*. Berkeley: University of California Press, 1974.
Merleau-Ponty, Maurice. "Husserl at the Limits of Phenomenology." In *Maurice Merleau-Ponty: Themes from the Lectures at the Collège de France, 1952–1960*, translated by John O'Neill, 113–23. Evanston: Northwestern University Press, 1970.

———. *The Phenomenology of Perception*. London and Henley: Routledge and Kegan Paul, 1962.

Michaelis, Johann David. *Introduction to the New Testament*. Translated by Herbert Marsh. London: Joseph Johnson, 1793.

———. "Proofs of the Authenticity of the New Testament." Translated anonymously. In *The Christian's Complete Family Bible*, 949–60. London: 1808.

Miller, Dan. "Blake and the Deconstructive Interlude." In *Blake and the Argument of Method*, edited by Dan Miller, Mark Bracher, and Donald Ault, 139–67. Durham and London: Duke University Press, 1987.

Miner, Earl. "Afterword." In *Literary Uses of Typology*, edited by Earl Miner, 370–94. Princeton: Princeton University Press, 1970.

———, ed. *Literary Uses of Typology*. Princeton: Princeton University Press, 1977.

Mitchell, W. J. T. *Blake's Composite Art*. Princeton: Princeton University Press, 1978.

———. "Dangerous Blake." *Studies in Romanticism* 21 (Fall 1982), 41–47.

———. "Style as Epistemology: Blake and the Movement toward Abstraction in Romantic Art." *Studies in Romanticism* 16 (Spring 1977): 145–64.

Murray, Roger. "Blake and the Ideal of Simplicity." *Studies in Romanticism* 13 (Spring 1974): 89–104.

"Nitsch's *Introductory View of Kant's Principles*." Review of *A general and introductory View of Professor Kant's Principles concerning Man, the World and the Deity, submitted to the Consideration of the Learned*, by F. A. Nitsch. *The Analytical Review* (January 1797): 11–23.

Nurmi, Martin. *Blake's Marriage of Heaven and Hell*. Kent: Kent State University Bulletin, 1957.

———. *William Blake*. Kent: Kent State University Bulletin, 1976.

O'Neill, Judith, ed. *Critics on Blake*. Coral Gables: University of Miami Press, 1986.

Ostriker, Alicia. "Dancing at the Devil's Party." *Critical Inquiry* 13 (Spring 1987): 3–14.

Otto, Peter. *Constructive Vision and Visionary Deconstruction: Los, Eternity, and the Productions of Time in the Later Poetry of William Blake*. Oxford: The Clarendon Press, 1991.

———. "The Spectrous Embrace, the Moment of Regeneration, and

Those Two Seventh Nights." *Colby Library Quarterly* 22 (September 1987): 135–43.

———. "Visionary Deconstruction: The Bard's Song in Blake's *Milton*." *Philological Quarterly* 66 (Spring 1987): 207–30.

Paley, Morton. *The Continuing City: William Blake's "Jerusalem."* Oxford: The Clarendon Press, 1983.

———. *William Blake*. Oxford: Phaidon Press, 1978.

Paley, Morton, and Michael Phillips, eds. *William Blake: Essays in Honour of Sir Geoffrey Keynes*. Oxford: The Clarendon Press, 1973.

Pechey, Graham. "*The Marriage of Heaven and Hell*: A Text and Its Conjuncture." *Oxford Literary Review* 3 (1979): 52–76.

Peckham, Morse. "Romanticism: The Present State of Theory." *The Triumph of Romanticism*. Columbia: University of South Carolina Press, 1970.

Peterfreund, Stuart. "Argument as Art, Argument as Science." *Studies in Eighteenth-Century Culture* 10, edited by Harry C. Payne, 205–26. Madison: University of Wisconsin Press, 1981.

———. "The Problem of Originality and Blake's *Poetical Sketches*." *English Literary History* 52 (1985): 673–705.

Pfau, Thomas. "Rhetoric and the Existential: Romantic Studies and the Question of the Subject." *Studies in Romanticism* 26 (Winter 1987): 487–512.

Piquet, François. "Blake, l'intertexte de *Jerusalem* et les tribulations d'Albion." *Romantisme* (1985): 35–46.

Poland, Lynn M. *Literary Criticism and Biblical Hermeneutics: A Critique of Formalist Approaches*. Chico, Calif.: Scholars Press, 1985.

Punter, David. "Blake: Creative and Uncreative Labour." *Studies in Romanticism* 16 (Fall 1977): 535–61.

———. *Blake, Hegel, and Dialectic*. Amsterdam: Editions Rodopi B.V., 1982.

Raine, Kathleen. *Blake and Tradition*. Princeton: Princeton University Press, 1968.

Rajan, Tilottama. "Displacing Post-Structuralism: Romantic Studies after Paul de Man." *Studies in Romanticism* (Winter 1985): 451–74.

———. "The Supplement of Reading." *New Literary History* 17 (Spring 1986): 573–94.

Rasmussen, David M., ed. *Mythic-Symbolic Language and Philosophical Anthropology*. The Hague, 1971.

Rawls, John. *A Theory of Justice.* Cambridge: The Belknap Press of Harvard University Press, 1971.

Read, Dennis. "The Context of Blake's 'Public Address': Cromek and the Chalcographic Society." *Philological Quarterly* 60 (Winter 1981): 69–86.

Reide, David G. "The Symbolism of the Loins in Blake's *Jerusalem*." *Studies in English Literature, 1500–1900* 21 (Autumn 1981): 547–63.

Ricoeur, Paul. "What Is a Text?" In *Mythic-Symbolic Language and Philosophical Anthropology,* edited by David M. Rasmussen, 135–52. The Hague, 1971.

Rose, Edward J. "Blake's *Jerusalem*, St. Paul, and Biblical Prophecy." *English Studies in Canada* 11 (December 1985): 396–412.

———. " 'Forms Eternal Exist For-ever': The Covenant of the Harvest in Blake's Prophetic Poems." In *Blake's Visionary Forms Dramatic,* edited by David V. Erdman and John E. Grant, 443–62. Princeton: Princeton University Press, 1970.

———. "The Structure of Blake's *Jerusalem*." *Bucknell Review* 11 (1963): 35–54.

Rosenfeld, Alvin H., ed. *William Blake: Essays for S. Foster Damon.* Providence: Brown University Press, 1969.

Rothenberg, Molly Anne. "Blake Reads 'The Bard': Contextual Displacement and Conditions of Readability in *Jerusalem*." *SEL: Studies in English Literature, 1500–1900* 27 (Summer 1987): 489–502.

———. "*Jerusalem*'s 'Forgotten Remembrances': A Blakean Analytic of Narrativity and Ideology." *Genre* 23 (Summer–Fall 1990): 205–26.

———. "The Provisional Vision of Blake's *Jerusalem*." *Word & Image* 3 (October–December 1987): 305–11.

Said, Edward. "The Problem of Textuality: Two Exemplary Positions." *Critical Inquiry* (Summer 1978): 673–714.

Schiff, Richard. "Representation, Copying, and the Technique of Originality." *New Literary History* 15 (Winter 1984): 333–63.

Schleifer, Ronald. "Simile, Metaphor, and Vision: Blake's Narration of Prophecy in *America*." *Studies in English Literature, 1500–1900* 19 (Autumn 1979): 569–87.

Schorer, Mark. *William Blake: The Politics of Vision.* New York: Vintage Books, 1959.

Shaffer, E. S. *"Kubla Khan" and The Fall of Jerusalem: The Mythological*

School in Biblical Criticism and Secular Literature, 1770–1880. Cambridge: Cambridge University Press, 1975.
Shaviro, Steven. " 'Striving with Systems': Blake and the Politics of Difference." In *Essential Articles for the Study of William Blake, 1970–1984*, edited by Nelson Hilton, 271–99. Hamden, Conn.: The Shoe String Press, 1986.
Sherry, Peggy Meyer. "The 'Predicament' of the Autograph: 'William Blake.'" *Glyph* 5: 131–55.
Stempel, Daniel. "Blake, Foucault, and the Classical Episteme." *PMLA* 96 (May 1981): 388–407.
Szondi, Peter. "Introduction to Literary Hermeneutics." *New Literary History* 10 (1978–1979): 17–29.
Tannenbaum, Leslie. *Biblical Tradition in Blake's Early Prophecies: The Great Code of Art.* Princeton: Princeton University Press, 1982.
Todorov, Tzvetan. *Mikhail Bakhtin: The Dialogical Principle.* Translated by Wlad Godzich. Minneapolis: University of Minnesota Press, 1984.
Vaughan, Frank A. "Blake's Illustrations to Gray's 'The Bard.'" *Colby Library Quarterly* 17 (December 1981): 211–37.
Vogler, Thomas A. "Intertextual Signifiers and the Blake of That Already." *Romanticism Past and Present* 9 (Winter 1985): 1–33.
———. "Re:Naming *MIL/TON*." In *Unnam'd Forms: Blake and Textuality*, edited by Nelson Hilton and Thomas A. Vogler, 141–76. Berkeley: University of California Press, 1986.
———. "The Tropology of Silence in Eighteenth-Century English Blank Verse." *The Eighteenth Century: Theory and Interpretation* 26 (1985): 211–37.
Warner, Janet. *Blake and the Language of Art.* Kingston, Ontario: McGill-Queens University Press, 1984.
Warner, Nicholas O. " 'The Eye Altering Alters All': Blake and Esthetic Perception." *Colby Library Quarterly* 19 (March 1983): 18–28.
Welch, Dennis M. "Imitation in Blake's *Night Thoughts* Illustrations." *Colby Library Quarterly* 22 (September 1986): 165–84.
White, Hayden. *The Content of the Form.* Baltimore: Johns Hopkins University Press, 1987.
———. " 'Figuring the Nature of the Times Deceased': Literary Theory and Historical Writing." Manuscript.

Witke, Joanne. "*Jerusalem*: A Synoptic Poem." *Comparative Literature* 32 (1970): 265–78.

Wittreich, Joseph Anthony, Jr. *Angel of Apocalypse*. Madison: University of Wisconsin Press, 1975.

———. "Opening the Seals." In *William Blake: Essays for S. Foster Damon*, edited by Alvin H. Rosenfeld. Providence: Brown University Press, 1969.

——— "Painted Prophecies." In *Blake in His Time*, edited by Robert N. Essick and Donald Pearce, 101–15. Bloomington: Indiana University Press, 1978.

Worrall, David. "Blake's *Jerusalem* and the Visionary History of Britain." *Studies in Romanticism* 16 (Spring 1977): 189–216.

Index

Absolutism, 2
Abstraction: Blake on, 84
Adams, Hazard, 88
Adulteress, Forgiven: and typology in *Jerusalem*, 104–5
Agency, 4, 71. *See also* Consciousness; Identity; Ideology; Individual; Mind; Perception; Possessive Selfhood; Subject; Subjectivity
Albion, 51–53, 56, 57, 58, 76, 91, 101, 106, 133*n*39; as phenomenalistic subject, 55*n*43, 90–91; fourfold, 56, 85, 91–97; misidentification of, 69, 71–79, 96, 113–28; refusal of Saviour, 72, 73–74; and oneness, 90–91
Allegory, 16; of Christianity in *Jerusalem*, 76*n*4
Althusser, Louis, 107
Analytical Review, The, 3, 44*n*37, 79. *See also* Geddes, Alexander; Godwin, William; Higher Criticism; Johnson, Joseph; Kant, Immanuel; Nitsch, F. A.; Paine, Thomas; Price, Richard; Priestley, Joseph
Annihilation: of possessive Selfhood, 85. *See also* Damrosch, Leopold; Possessive Selfhood
Antimetaphysics: and Kant, 82*n*9; in Blake, 108–28
Antinarrative, 108. *See also* Narrative
Antiphrasis: in Augustinian hermeneutics, 66
Apocalypse: in *Jerusalem*, 85, 109, 137
Apostles: Acts of, 15; in Blake, 28. *See also* Bible; Parable
Aristotle: Blake's allusions to, 21–22
Arthur, King of England: in Blake, 101
Association psychology: Blake's response to, 6, 120; and memory, 118; and identity, 126. *See also* Hartley, David; Hume, David; Identity; Memory
Augustine, St., 13, 65–78; *Confessions*, 65*n*1; Blake's revision of, 66–78, 82; on subjectivity, 98; *De Doctrina Christiana*, 66*n*1, 87*n*15
Ault, Donald: on Blake's textuality, 2, 3, 3*n*1, 5*n*2, 20*n*17, 42*n*33, 112–13; on poetic authority, 9*n*2
Authenticity, 21; of Bible, 22
Authority, 5, 6, 9–12, 17, 25–36, 37, 59, 65, 68, 76, 77, 78, 82, 90, 111, 112, 119, 121–22, 124–25, 137; Blake's subversion of, 5, 17; Blake's view of, 21–22, 67, 78; in Matthew, 27–34; and Jesus, 28; in Augustine, 67
Authorship, 22; Blake on, 47.*See also* Authority; Higher Criticism

Bacon, Francis, 5; in Blake scholarship, 99*n*23
Bakhtin, Mikhail, 132–33. *See also* Dialogism; Narrativity
Bard: in Gray, 53–56; suicide of, 56–57
Barthes, Roland, 1; and textuality, 129–33, 136
Belief: conditions of, 22, 24, 30
Bible: authority of, 5, 20, 22, 36, 47; and Blake criticism, 6; authenticity/authorship of, 12, 12*n*3, 19–20, 19*n*15, 22; interpretation of, 12, 13, 22, 24, 58, 59–61, 65, 98*n*22; as literature, 13, 20; unity of, 13, 20, 59–61; truth of, 14; as revision, 16; as rhetoric, 17–18, 20, 59–61; as self-authorizing, 27–28; Blake's revision of, 35; Augustine's interpretive method for, 65–68, 72; and typology, 98, 105
Biblical criticism: in eighteenth century, 12–13; Blake's response to, 12, 18–27. *See also* Blake, his use of Bible; Higher Criticism
Blake, William: scholarship on, 1, 2, 4, 5*n*2, 6, 11, 65*n*1, 70, 76, 88; his historical context, 1–6, 12; use of chaos, 2, 6; on Milton, 9, 26; definition of

155

inspiration, 18–27; and Joseph Johnson, 19; defense of Paine, 20, 24, 37, 105; allusions to Aristotle, 21–22; and Howes, 22–23, 22n18; on miracles, 24; knowledge of Newton, 25–26; knowledge of Pareus, 26; self-described as wicked, 32–33; definition of righteousness, 32–35; knowledge of Geddes, 42; knowledge of Price, Paine, and Godwin, 44n37; on authorship, 47; knowledge of Kant, 80n6; heaven and hell in, 85n11; on history, 99–101

—his epistemology: and eighteenth-century philosophy, 1–6, 116–20; as critique of metaphysics, 1, 5, 46–47, 82n9, 106, 108–28, 129; relation to poststructuralism, 1–3, 6, 45, 129–37; and ideological mediation, 1, 21n17, 37, 43, 45, 107, 109–10, 134; philosophical coherence of, 2; of intentionality, 2, 45, 56, 96; relation to skepticism, 3, 4, 82–84, 116–18; radicalism of, 3, 37, 65, 133–37; and authority, 5, 6, 20; and constitution of subjectivity, 6; relation to phenomenology, 6, 88; relation to association psychology, 6, 120, 126; relation to Higher Criticism, 18–27, 37–38, 65; on truth and error, 20n17, 45–46, 78, 132; compared to Hume's, 37, 112, 116–18, 120; and perceptual mediation, 43, 45; and particularity, 46–47; of determinate meaning, 59–61, 112–28; relation to Augustinian hermeneutics, 65–78; and solipsism, 82–84; as critique of Kant's philosophy, 82–84, 107–8, 118; of spatiotemporality, 83; and abstraction, 84; and individuality, 84–87; and universality, 91; compared to Comte's, 112; of causality, 116–18, 121–22, 123–38; and transcendental subject, 118–28; its political implications, 133–37

—his textual practice: compared to poststructuralism, 1–3, 6, 45, 129–37; and intertextuality, 2, 3, 53, 127–28; as radical Christianity, 4; as critique of metaphysics, 5, 46–47, 113–28; and textuality, 6, 68, 129–37; as construction of inspiration, 18–27; as disseminating authority, 33–36; contextual displacement in, 33–36, 56, 78, 96, 126; as graphic representation, 40–43, 46–47, 70–71; textual variants in, 42; as ideological analysis, 45, 134; and representation, 46–47; and particularity, 46–47; as imitation, 46–47, 47n38; citation of Gray's "The Bard," 53–58; as revisionary strategy, 65; as revision of Augustinian hermeneutics, 65n1, 66–78, 82; close reading of, 70–71, 90–97, 113–28; function of transcendental signifiers in, 72–78, 105, 109, 111, 119–20; as revision of typology, 98–109; as narrative analysis, 108–28; function of Urizen in, 131

—his use of Bible: as radical Christian, 4; relation to Higher Criticism, 5, 6, 18–27, 37–38, 65; and rhetoric, 18; as record of oppression, 18; and Coleridge, 18; as literature, 20; and prophecy, 22–23, 22n18, 25–26; and Great Code of Art, 24; Revelation, 26; Gospels, 28–36; and parable of sheep and goats, 32–37; as revision, 35; compared to Dissenters' interpretation, 37; Deuteronomy, 59–61; compared to Augustine, 65n1, 66–78, 82; as revision of Christian hermeneutics, 68–78; as revision of typology, 98–108

—*Jerusalem*, 1–6, 10, 11; textuality of, 2, 4, 111–28, 129–37; and chaos, 2, 6, 49, 136–37; problem of poetic authority in, 9–12, 37; Plate 4, 9n1, 10, 56, 58, 68–69, 71–78; Plate 3, address "To the Public," 10, 11, 22, 22n18, 28, 37, 38, 42–43; problem of authorship of, 10–11, 37, 42–43; syntactical uncertainties in, 10–12, 70–71; as self-cited text, 11, 49; and inspiration, 19, 22, 22n18, 42–43; and Revelation, 26; and parable of sheep and goats, 28–36; and Higher Criticism, 37–38; compared to *Masora*, 38–40; graphic reading of, 42–43, 70–71, 89n17, 91–97, 112–13; contextual displacement in, 48–53; Plate 98, 49–50; Plates 94–97, 51–52, 53, 54–55n43, 89n17; effect of troping in, 52–53; Plates 5 and 94 compared to "The Task," 54–55n43; Plates 95 and 96 compared to "The Bard," 57–58; as narratival metacommentary, 70–71, 108–10, 129, 132; Christian interpretation of, 71–78; and resemblance of mind and world,

Index

82; and subjectivity, 83; and annihilation of possessive Selfhood, 85; Plate 97, 89*n*17, 90, 91–97; and typology, 101*n*2, 103–8; Plate 42, 102; Plates 61 and 62, 103–5; Plate 90, 106; as deconstruction of metaphysics, 111–28, 129, 132; Plate 29/33, 113–28; causality in, 116–18, 121–22, 123–28; and construction of ontology, 129; and error, 132; and Hobbes, 134*n*40
—other works of: *The Four Zoas*, 2, 3, 3*n*1, 42*n*33, 112–13; *The Marriage of Heaven and Hell*, 9, 10, 18; "Annotations to Watson's *Apology*," 20–24, 105; *Laocoon*, 24, 102; notebook manuscripts, 32*n*24; *A Vision of the Last Judgment*, 43; *A Descriptive Catalogue*, 46, 99–101, 101*n*24; *Milton*, 85; *The Ancient Britons*, 100
—*See also* Bible; Metaphysics; Parable; Prophecy; Subject; Subjectivity
Bloom, Harold, 74, 120
Bounding line, 46–48
Breadth: Merleau-Ponty's analysis of, 95–96. *See also* Phenomenology
Breath Divine: in *Jerusalem*, 51
Bride: as typological subject in *Jerusalem*, 104–5
Brittannia: in *Jerusalem*, 51–52

Carr, Stephen Leo, 41–42, 41*n*30
Causality: in *Jerusalem*, 116–18, 121–22, 123–28. *See also* Association psychology; Hume, David; Kant, Immanuel; Identity; Memory; Narrativity
Chaos: in *Jerusalem*, 2, 6, 49, 136–37; theory of, 2, 137; and representation, 47; definitions of, 136–37. *See also* Determinacy
Charity: as message of Bible, 77
Christ: miracles of, 24, 30; and interpretive authority, 31–33; identity assumed in interpretations of *Jerusalem*, 69; and typology, 98–108; as ideological function in Blake, 107; as "Ratio" in Blake, 107–8. *See also* Jesus; Saviour; Signifier, transcendental
Christian: reader, 65–68; subjects, 68; Muse, 71; doctrine, 97. *See also* Augustine, St.; Inner Light philosophy; Unitarians
Christianity: Blake as radical, 4; values of, 69; and salvation, 74, 109; doctrine of identification in Christ, 77; and narrative, 111. *See also* Augustine, St.; Inner Light philosophy; Unitarians
Citationality, 49, 58–61; in Gray's "The Bard," 53
Civil War, English: and subversion of authority, 5, 78
Coleridge, Samuel Taylor: and Higher Criticism, 12*n*3, 17, 17*n*12, 18; views on Bible compared to Blake's, 18; *Biographia Literaria*, 79, 79*n*5
Conjunction, constant: in Hume, 117. *See also* Blake, his epistemology; Blake, his textual practice; Causality; Hume, David; Identity; Narrativity
Consciousness, 4, 50. *See also* Agency; Identity; Ideology; Individual; Mind; Perception; Possessive Selfhood; Subject; Subjectivity
Contextual displacement: as condition of signification in *Jerusalem*, 48–52. *See also* Citationality; Rhetoric; Tropology
Covenant of Priam, 110
Custom: in Hume, 108, 116–18

Damrosch, Leopold, 84–87, 85*n*11, 87*n*15, 91, 133*n*39; *Symbol and Truth in Blake's Myth*, 84–87, 87*n*15
Deconstruction: relation to Blake, 6; of immanence, 43; of perception, 45; and politics, 134. *See also* Antimetaphysics; Blake, William, his epistemology; Derrida, Jacques; Dissemination; Poststructuralism
Democratization, 58–59
Depth: Merleau-Ponty's analysis of, 95–96
Derrida, Jacques, 49, 52*n*40. *See also* Deconstruction; Poststructuralism
Descriptive Catalog, A. See Blake, William, other works of
Design: as Blake's term for inspiration, 19–27. *See also* Inspiration
Desire: as liberating, 9
Determinacy, 45–46, 47, 48, 58, 66, 71, 96–97, 110, 112, 120, 129–30, 135; in Bible, 59–60; Blake's criticism of, 61, 112. *See also* Blake, his epistemology; Chaos; Metaphysics
Deterministic reason: Blake's critique of, 1. *See also* Determinacy; Kant, Immanuel

Devil: in parable of temptation in wilderness, 34
Devouring Power, 123–24
Dialogism, 77; Bakhtin's, 127–28, 132–33
Difference: and identity, 66
Dimensionality: in conditions of representation, 92–97
Discourse, 5, 78, 83, 108–28; historiographic, 101; and custom, 108; contested, 127–28. *See also* Narrativity; Textuality
Displacement, 33–36, 48–49, 51, 56, 58, 59, 78, 96, 111, 136; and Albion, 56; of Jesus in Matthew, 60. *See also* Metonymy; Transfiguration; Tropology
Dissemination, 27, 33–36, 67, 106, 111. *See also* Antimetaphysics; Authority
Dissenters: interpretive stance of, 37
Divine: right, 5; Body, 32–33; will, 68; Voice, 73; Vision, 73, 113–28; Names, 106
Divinity: designated by canonical article, 39–40; in Christian tradition, 71; Albion's knowledge of, 72; in *Jerusalem*, 73–74, 105, 109, 111, 119–20; identity of, 119–20. *See also* Antimetaphysics; Metaphysics; Signifier, transcendental

Economics, 44; in *The Analytical Review*, 44n37
Edward the First, 53, 54, 56
Eichhorn, Johann Gottfried, 14n6; definition of inspiration, 16–17. *See also* Higher Criticism
Emanation: in *Jerusalem*, 52–53, 53n42, 124–28; identity of, 76, 124–28
Empiricism, 79, 83, 84, 120. *See also* Blake, his epistemology; Hume, David; Kant, Immanuel; Skepticism
England: in *Jerusalem*, 51–52
Enlightenment, 2, 4, 79
Enunciation: subject of, 58
Epic: voice, 10, 71; argument, 70, 71, 72; Christian, 71; poem, 119
Epistemology, 1, 2, 78, 106, 112. *See also* Association psychology; Blake, his epistemology; Empiricism; Hume, David; Kant, Immanuel; Phenomenology; Philosophy
Erdman, David: and punctuation of *Jerusalem*, 9n1, 120; interpretation of Plate 97, 95n19
Error: and truth, 45–46; production of, 78; and narrative form, 132. *See also* Antimetaphysics; Metaphysics; Blake, his epistemology; Truth
Essick, Robert, 40–43, 41n30. *See also* Blake, his textual practice
Eternal Death, 71, 73
Eternal Life: in *Jerusalem*, 71
Eternity, 85; in *Jerusalem*, 111
Ethos: Blake's use of, 21
Evil: Augustine on, 65

Fabrication: as Blake's term for inspiration, 19–27. *See also* Inspiration
Feminism: poststructuralist, 6
Fiction: Blake compares to history, 100–101
Formalism, 49
Four Zoas, The. See Blake, William, other works of
Frei, Hans, 13, 98n22
Frye, Northrop, 43–44, 85n11
"Furnaces of Affliction," 57

Gabler, Johann Philipp, 14n6, 15. *See also* Higher Criticism
Gadamer, Hans-Georg, 35
Geddes, Alexander: translations of the Bible, 3, 38; proponent of Higher Criticism, 19; works of, 19n15; Blake's knowledge of, 38; on interpreting the *Masora*, 38–42; and semiotics, 40; "fragment hypothesis," 41; views on textual variants compared to Blake's, 42. *See also* Higher Criticism
Gender: as textual effect in *Jerusalem*, 112, 125
Geneva canon, 39–40
God: writing in name of, 22; intention of, 37; word of, 47, 60; as determinant of meaning, 59–61; in *Paradise Lost*, 102–3; production of, 112; definition of, 121, 121n34. *See also* Metaphysics; Signifier, transcendental
Godwin, William, 44, 44n37
Gospels, 12, 15; Blake's use of, 28–36; and typology, 98n22. *See also* Apostles; Higher Criticism; Inspiration
Gray, Thomas: and "The Bard," 3, 53–58; "The Bard" compared to Cowper's "The Task," 55n43

Haraway, Donna, 135
Harlot: as typological subject in *Jerusalem*, 104–5

Index

Hartley, David: his theory of subjectivity, 79, 120; Hume's relation to, 120*n*33. *See also* Association psychology; Hume, David; Memory
Hebrew: poetry, 14; patriarchs, 101. *See also* Lowth, Robert
Hegemony: and subjectivity, 78
Hermaphroditic Albion, 125
Hermeneutics: biblical, 12*n*3, 21; Augustinian, 13, 65, 68, 98; displacement by rhetoric, 17–18, 67, 77; status as inspired, 22; and the construction of authority, 27; of correct interpretations, 34–35; traditional, 35–36, 43, 67–68; and referentiality, 43; Ricoeur on, 52; and determinate meaning, 59; Blake's revision of, 65–78; closed, 67; and hegemony, 68; and typology, 106. *See also* Augustine, St.; Blake, his use of Bible; Higher Criticism
Higher Criticism, 12, 13–18, 24; Blake's knowledge of, 5, 12*n*3, 18–27, 19*n*16, 22, 37–38, 65; Joseph Johnson and, 12*n*3, 14*n*6; impact on Blake's definition of inspiration, 18–27; and *Jerusalem*, 37–38; and multiple motivations of biblical texts, 45; and typology, 101. *See also* Blake, his use of Bible; Eichhorn, Johann Gottfried; Frei, Hans; Gabler, Johann Philipp; Inspiration; Michaelis, Johann David; Shaffer, E. S.; Tannenbaum, Leslie
Hilton, Nelson, 2, 41*n*30, 53*n*42. *See also* Poststructuralism; Textuality
History: Whig, 100*n*23; Blake compares to fiction, 100–101; as *kairos* vs. *chronos*, 101; production of, 112
Hobbes, Thomas, 78, 84, 134*n*40
Holy-Ghost, 9
Holy-One, 73, 74, 76. *See also* Signifier, transcendental
Horizon: in Husserl, 89–90. *See also* Phenomenology
Howes, Thomas: commentary on Bishop Lowth's *Lectures*, 15; Tannenbaum's discussion of, 16*n*9, 22*n*18; on disunity as sign of inspiration, 22–23; on prophetic style, 23; on oratorical order of prophecy, 25. *See also* Inspiration
"Human Form": in *Jerusalem*, 122–23
Human Form Divine: in *Jerusalem*, 102, 106
Humanism: Enlightenment, 4, 79

Hume, David: Blake's agreement with, 37; and authority, 79; and theory of subjectivity, 79, 126; and Coleridge, 79*n*5; and skepticism, 81*n*7; Kant's objections to, 82, 82*n*9; and skeptical empiricism, 83; as Blakean signifier, 99*n*23; compared to Kant, 108, 117–18; and metaphysics, 112; on custom, 116–18, 128*n*35; on causality, identity, and memory, 116–20; and narrative, 117; and association psychology, 120*n*33; his deconstruction of the subject, 126. *See also* Association psychology; Empiricism; Kant, Immanuel; Memory; Philosophy; Skepticism; Subjectivity
Husserl, Edmund, 83, 88–91, 89*n*17. *See also* Perception; Phenomenology; Subject, phenomenalistic

Iconicity: Carr's views of, 42
Idealism: in review of Nitsch, 80; and Blake criticism, 84–87
Ideality, 37
Identity, 6, 52, 56, 66–67, 72–73; Albion's, 74–78; Damrosch on, 84–87; as problem in *Jerusalem*, 113–28; and gender, 125; and narrative, 129. *See also* Christ; Ideology; Individual; Jesus; Perception; Possessive Selfhood; Saviour; Subject; Subjectivity
Ideology, 1, 37, 43, 44, 45, 77, 107, 109–10, 109*n*28, 112, 113, 113*n*29; Blake's analysis of, 134. *See also* Hegemony; Marx, Karl; Perception; Subject; Subjectivity
Imagination: relationship to reality in Blake, 43–44
Imitation: Blake on, 46–47, 47*n*38
Immanence: and "Inner Light" doctrine, 37; Essick on, 42–43; Blake's deconstruction of, 43; criticized, 47
Immediacy: and particularity, 47
Indeterminacy: textual, 40, 41, 70–71; and law, 75; of object, 89–90. *See also* Determinacy; Textuality
Individual: particularity of, 47; Hobbes's description of, 79; Blake on, 84–87; as limit of contraction, 111. *See also* Consciousness; Identity; Ideology; Limit of Contraction; Perception; Possessive Selfhood; Subject; Subjectivity
Inner Light philosophy, 5, 37, 43

Inspiration, 9–18; as function of rhetoric, 17–18, 21; Blake's definitions of, 18–27. *See also* Higher Criticism

Intentionality: Blake's criticism of, 2, 45, 96; originary, 21; of God, 37; and bounding lines, 47; and poststructuralism, 48–49; as equation of origin and meaning, 51; and Albion, 56; and citationality, 58; authorial, 61; divine, 61; and Husserl, 89*n*17. *See also* Authority; Determinacy; Metaphysics; Referentiality; Textuality

Interpretation, 16, 25, 35, 36, 37, 43; of the *Masora*, 38; biblical, 65; Christian, 65–78; of *Jerusalem*, Plate 4, from Christian viewpoint, 71–78. *See also* Hermeneutics; Higher Criticism

Intertextuality: and *Jerusalem*, 2, 3, 53, 127–28, 134*n*40. *See also* Dialogism; Textuality

Intratextuality, 2, 3, 35

Irony: as trope of identity, 66

Israelites, 59, 60

Jehovah, 111

Jerusalem, character in *Jerusalem*: as author of poem, 11; daughters of, 73, 76; identity of, 76, 124–28; as typological subject, 104–5; and Vala, 126–27, 135. *See also* Emanation

Jerusalem. *See* Blake, William, *Jerusalem*

Jesus: source of his authority questioned, 28–34; as interpretive authority, 30–36; temptation in wilderness, 34, 58–61; as Los in *Jerusalem*, 52; and typology, 98*n*22, 102. *See also* Augustine, St.; Christ; Hermeneutics; Saviour; Signifier, transcendental

Johnson, Joseph: and Kant, 3, 79, 80*n*6; publisher of Higher Critics, 12, 14*n*6, 29; friendship with Blake, 19; publisher of Geddes, 19*n*15; publisher of Price, Paine, and Godwin, 44*n*37

Joseph, character in *Jerusalem*: as typological subject, 104

Kant, Immanuel: and deterministic reason, 1; and transcendental subjectivity, 1, 81*n*7, 82–83, 117, 125; and Johnson's *The Analytical Review*, 3, 79; and transcendental idealism, 5, 6, 82*n*9; Nitsch's summary and translation of, 79–82; Blake's knowledge of, 80*n*6; and skepticism, 81*n*7, 84, 112; his categories, 81–82, 89; response to Hume, 82, 82*n*9, 100*n*23, 112, 116, 117–18; on practical reason, 82; and metaphysics, 82*n*9; Blake's agreement with, 82–83; Blake's rejection of, 82–84, 91; and phenomenology, 83, 88; description of reason, 107–8; and causality, 117; and memory, 117. *See also* Blake, his epistemology; Hume, David; Identity; Memory; Philosophy; Spatiotemporality; Subjectivity, transcendental

Kermode, Frank, 34–35

Language, 5, 53–58, 61, 65, 67–68, 78, 98; Augustine on, 65–68; as Logos, 98. *See also* Augustine, St.; Hermeneutics; Perception; Referentiality; Rhetoric; Tropology

Laocoon. *See* Blake, William, other works of

Liberty: linked to oppression, 1, 35; and desire, 9; and ideology, 77; and textuality, 129–33

Life of Immortality: defined, 109, 111

Limitation: necessity of, 68, 90–91, 131–32, 134–36. *See also* Limit of Contraction; Perception; Subject, phenomenalistic; Urizen

Limit of Contraction: defined, 90, 134, 136

Locke, John: his theory of subjectivity, 79; on authority, 79; as Blakean signifier, 99*n*23. *See also* Authority; Empiricism; Hume, David; Skepticism; Subjectivity

Los: as Jesus in *Jerusalem*, 52; on universal attributes, 106; on Satan, 107; identity in *Jerusalem*, 113

Lowth, Bishop Robert: on biblical style, 14, 23; Howes's commentary on his *Lectures*, 15; and typology, 98*n*22

McGann, Jerome, 2, 5*n*2, 9*n*2, 18, 41

Mann, Paul, 2, 5*n*2, 113*n*29

Manna: as biblical trope, 60

Marriage of Heaven and Hell, The. *See* Blake, William, other works of

Marx, Karl, 134

Mary: as typological subject in *Jerusalem*, 104–5

Masora, 38–42

Index

Materialism: in Nitsch's review of Kant, 80
Materiality: and interpretive limitation, 47
Matthew: and problem of authority, 28–36; temptation in wilderness, 59. *See also* Apostles; Authority; Christ; Jesus; Moses; Satan
Meaning: production of, 2, 56, 59–61, 96; and determinacy, 36, 112, 130, 136; as identity, 52; theory in Gray's "The Bard," 52–58. *See also* Authority; Determinacy; Referentiality; Rhetoric; Tropology
Mediation: ideological, 1, 37, 43–48, 68, 109–10, 134; of perception, 37, 43–48, 68, 109–10, 134; between individual and society, 134. *See also* Ideology; Perception
Memory: "Unformd," 115–20; in Hume, 115–20; in eighteenth-century philosophy, 116–20; and causality, 117. *See also* Association psychology; Hume, David; Kant, Immanuel; Locke, John
Merleau-Ponty, Maurice: on phenomenology of spatiotemporal perception, 95
Metaphysics: Blake's critique of, 1, 5, 106, 108, 111, 129; of authority, 21, 137; Kant's criticism of, 82$n9$; of transcendental subject, 118; grounding of, 123; in eighteenth-century philosophy, 128. *See also* Authority; Hermeneutics; Hume, David; Kant, Immanuel; Referentiality; Rhetoric; Tropology; Skepticism
Metonymy: as trope of displacement, 51, 56
Michaelis, Johann David, 13–14; *Einleitung*, 13$n6$; Marsh's translation of, 14$n6$; Johnson's publication of, 14$n6$, 19, 19$n15$. *See also* Higher Criticism
Mill, James, 83
Milton, John: and inspiration, 9; writings on Pareus, 26; allusions to *Paradise Lost* in *Jerusalem*, 70, 102–3; and tradition, 71
Milton. See Blake, William, other works of
Mind, 77–78. *See also* Subjectivity
Miracles, 24, 30. *See also* Belief, conditions of; Rhetoric
Monologism: 133, 134$n40$, 136

Moral Law: and Albion, 60, 75, 83, 90; and Moses, 60; and Kant, 82, 83. *See also* Metaphysics
Moral Philosophy, 5
Moses: writing in the name of, 22; and contextual displacement, 59–61
Multiplicity: and Satan, 123

Naming, 52–53, 53
Narrative: Blake's analytics of, 112, 130–33. *See also* Narrativity; Referentiality
Narrativity, 107, 109–28, 109$n28$, 130–33; and Hume, 117. *See also* Narrative; Textuality
Nature: in Gray's "The Bard," 53–58; and Vala, 128
New Testament, 16, 28; Blake's revision of, 58–61. *See also* Bible
Newton: on form of prophecy, 25, 25$n21$; as Blakean signifier, 99$n23$; and definitions of God, 121$n34$
Nitsch, F. A.: translation and summary of Kant, 79–82, 80$n6$, 81$n7$, 105, 107–8. *See also* Kant, Immanuel; Philosophy, eighteenth-century
Noema, 89

Object: and subject, 79–83, 89–90, 111. *See also* Blake, his epistemology; Empiricism; Hume, David; Kant, Immanuel; Skepticism
Old Testament, 15, 23, 98$n22$. *See also* Bible
Ontology, 76, 112. *See also* Blake, his epistemology; Metaphysics
Oppression: links to liberty, 1; production of, 35, 68; resistance to, 78; and possessive Selfhood, 82
Optic ray, central, 92–94. *See also* Perception
Oratory: and prophecy, 22–23, 22$n18$

Paine, Thomas, 19–20; on ideological use of language, 21$n17$; *The Age of Reason*, 24; Blake's agreement with, 37, 105; on property rights, 44; published by Johnson, 44$n37$
Parable: of sheep and goats, 28–37, 73; as self-contradictory, 31–32. *See also* Bible; Blake, William, his use of Bible
Pareus: his commentary on prophecy, 26, 27$n22$
Particularity, 46–47

Pathos: Blake's use of, 21
Pentateuch, 13, 27–28. *See also* Authorship; Bible; Higher Criticism
Perception, 1, 5, 37, 43–48, 50, 59–61, 68, 109–10; limitation of, 59–61, 90, 95–97, 116, 126; primacy of individual, 84; definitions of, 89*n*17. *See also* Ideology; Limit of Contraction; Perspective; Possessive Selfhood; Referentiality; Subject; Subjectivity
Perspective, 94–97; systems of, 92–97
Pharisees, 29–30. *See also* Authority; Blake, his use of Bible; Parable
Phenomenology: relation to Blake's practice, 6, 88–91, 94–97; and radical empiricism, 83; as Damrosch's method, 86–87; and Poulet, 87, 87*n*15; Adams on, 88; Husserlian, 88–90; and Kant, 88; Merleau-Ponty, 95–96. *See also* Subject, phenomenalistic
Philosophy: eighteenth-century, 1, 2, 3, 78–82, 106, 112, 116–20; of radical feminism, 6; of mind, 78; nonempirical, 82*n*9; moral, 128; political, 128, 133–34; liberal, 134. *See also* Association psychology; Blake, William, his epistemology; Deconstruction; Empiricism; Epistemology; Hume, David; Husserl, Edmund; Kant, Immanuel; Ontology; Merleau-Ponty, Maurice; Metaphysics; Phenomenology; Poststructuralism; Skepticism; Solipsism
Poet: knowledge of source of authority, 9; "true," 9–10, 9*n*2; epistemological status of authority of, 11
Point of view: limited vs. transcendent, 55*n*43; God's, 61. *See also* Subject
Politics, 4, 6; and Blakean textuality, 133–37; and poststructuralism, 134
Possessive Selfhood: language of, 58–61, 133; and multiplicity, 74; and domination, 76; and hierarchy, 76; annihilation of, 85; deconstructed, 90–91. *See also* Identity; Perception; Phenomenology; Referentiality; Subject, phenomenalistic; Subjectivity
Poststructuralism, 1, 2, 4, 6, 48, 129–33, 133–37
Price, Richard, 44, 44*n*37
Priestley, Joseph, 19, 19*n*5, 44
Prophecy, 15–17, 22–24, 22*n*18, 25–26, 27, 29; as interpretation, 16, 25–26, 27; and rhetoric, 17, 23–24, 27; Howes on, 22–23; and typology, 102

Quakers, 5

Radicalism, 3, 4, 5, 44; Blake's, 55
Rationalism: in review of Nitsch, 80
Rationality, 2
Rationalization, 2
Readability, 48, 49, 51
Reader, 23*n*18, 67, 72
Reading, 58, 92
Real, the, 77
Reality, 82, 83. *See also* Epistemology; Metaphysics; Ontology
Reason: evaluation of, 108
Redemption, 77, 84
Referentiality, 42, 43, 48–49, 51, 52, 53, 56, 59–61, 78, 97; and Gray's "The Bard," 53–58; and possessive Selfhood, 58, 59–61. *See also* Hermeneutics; Narrative; Rhetoric; Subject, phenomenalistic; Tropology
Representation, 46–47, 92–97
Revelation, 12; in Augustine, 67
Revelation, Book of: Blake's use of, 26; textual reproduction of, 28. *See also* Bible
Revision, 5, 25; Blake's strategies of, 65
Rhetoric, 17–18, 22, 23–24, 56, 68, 86, 97–98; and interpretation of *Jerusalem*, 2, 68; Ricoeur on, 52; and Albion in *Jerusalem*, 56. *See also* Hermeneutics; Referentiality; Tropology
Ricoeur, Paul, 52, 61
Righteousness, 30–33
Rights: individual vs. natural, 5
Romanticism: and inspiration, 26

Sacred texts, 13–18, 25–26, 34–35, 98*n*22
Salvation, 74
Satan: as Blakean signifier, 5; identified with Christ in *Jerusalem*, 107
Saviour, character in *Jerusalem*, 5, 10, 11, 55*n*43, 58, 69, 71–78, 105
Schleiermacher, Friedrich Ernst Daniel, 17, 17*n*12
Shaffer, E. S., 13, 17. *See also* Higher Criticism
Sign, 42–43, 55, 61
Signification, 48–52, 53, 58, 65, 68, 69–70, 110. *See also* Referentiality
Signified: relation to signifier, 40. *See also* Geddes, Alexander; Hermeneutics; *Masora*; Referentiality; Signifier; Textuality; Tropology
Signifier: transcendental, 5, 47, 65, 67,

Index

68, 72, 77, 120, 124*n*40, 127–28; relation to signified, 40; shifting, 71. *See also* Geddes, Alexander; Hermeneutics; *Masora*; Referentiality; Signified; Textuality; Tropology
Similitude, 56; Augustine's view of, 66
"Single vision," 112
Sinners: creation of, 105
Skepticism, 3, 4, 6; radical implications of, 79, 82–84, 100*n*23, 108, 126, 128*n*35; in review of Nitsch, 81; liberatory potential of, 83–84; Kant on, 84, 116, 117–18; and Hume, 100*n*23, 112, 116, 117–18, 128*n*35; relation to positivism, 112; and identity, 116, 117–18; and memory, 117–18. *See also* Empiricism; Hume, David; Identity; Memory
Solipsism: and Kant, 81–84, 108; Blake's defense against, 83, 84, 108; Damrosch on, 84–87; typological defense against, 98
Son of Man: in parable of sheep and goats, 31–33; transcendental status of, 32; in typology, 102. *See also* Christ; Jesus; Signifier, transcendental
Space, 95, 115–16. *See also* Kant, Immanuel; Phenomenology; Spatiotemporality; Time
Spatiotemporality, 97, 115–28. *See also* Kant, Immanuel; Phenomenology
Spectre: of Reason, 52; in *Milton*, 85; as Blakean signifier, 121–28; as disorder, 129; in Damrosch, 133*n*39
Spectrous Chaos: as Blakean signifier, 113–28
Spectrous Dead: as Blakean signifier, 115
Spirit of Jesus: Blake's definition of, 33–34
Spiritualism: in review of Nitsch, 80
Subject, 1, 2, 4, 6, 56, 58, 59–61, 67, 68, 78, 83, 88, 90–97, 97–108, 108–28, 131, 135, 136–37; defined tropologically, 52; phenomenalistic, 55*n*43, 59–61, 78, 82, 83, 85, 88, 91–97, 110, 132, 136; and object, 79–83, 89–90, 111; Hume's deconstruction of, 126. *See also* Discourse; Feminism; Identity; Ideology; Individual; Mind; Perception; Possessive selfhood; Subjectivity; Tropology

Subjectivity: production of, 1, 6, 67, 68, 75, 78, 85, 90–91, 111–12; transcendental, 61, 91, 108, 118–28; eighteenth-century theories of, 79, 112; and *Jerusalem*, 83; transformation of, 83, 91–96; discursive formation of, 83, 98–99, 110–11; Christian doctrine of, 98; varying in Blake, 110–11; deconstructed, 116; intertextual, 116; limitations of, 136–37. *See also* Discourse; Feminism; Identity; Ideology; Individual; Perception; Possessive Selfhood; Subject; Tropology
Substitution: metonymic, 56
Systematicity, 1, 131–33

Tabula rasa: in *Jerusalem*, 120. *See also* Association psychology; Locke, John; Hume, David; Memory; Subjectivity, production of
Tannenbaum, Leslie, 9*n*2; on Howes, 15, 22–23; on biblical coherence, 16*n*9; on Blake's use of disunity, 22*n*18; on Blake's address "To the Public," 22*n*18; on Blake's use of typology, 101–2. *See also* Inspiration; Bible, unity of; Blake, his use of Bible; Howes, Thomas; Typology
Teleology: in Augustine's hermeneutics, 67; narratival, 71, 112–28
Temporality: of ideology, 107. *See also* Kant, Immanuel; Merleau-Ponty, Maurice; Phenomenology; Space; Spatiotemporality; Time
Textuality: Blake's vs. poststructuralism, 1–2, 6, 37, 68, 113–28; effect of subversion of authority, 11–12, 21; Essick on, 40; Blake's graphic, 40–43; ignored by Damrosch, 86; in Barthes, 129–32
Textual variants, 38–42. *See also* Authorship; Bible, unity of; Geddes, Alexander; Higher Criticism; McGann, Jerome
Time: and space, 95; and subjectivity, 97; creation of, 115–16, 125–26. *See also* Hume, David; Kant, Immanuel; Phenomenology; Spatiotemporality; Subject, phenomenalistic; Temporality
Todorov, Tzvetan, 132–33. *See also* Dialogism; Discourse; Monologism
Transcendence: in Blake scholarship, 4
Transcendentals: function in eighteenth-century philosophy, 6;

appeal to, 21; secularized, 24; Blake's construction of, 46–47, 67; as stabilizing meaning, 97; necessity of, 132. *See also* Metaphysics; Signifier; Subjectivity, transcendental

Transfiguration, 56, 58, 68. *See also* Displacement; Rhetoric; Tropology

Tropology, 51–53, 55, 56, 96–97; Albion's reliance on, 56; and determinacy, 58, 96–97; and biblical authority, 59–61; Augustine on, 65–68; double nature of, 66; and oppression, 68; and ideology, 77; Blake's emphasis on, 109–11. *See also* Albion; Augustine, St.; Authority; Blake, textual practice of; Determinacy; Displacement; Perception; Referentiality

Truth, 21, 67; Blake's philosophy of, 45–46. *See also* Metaphysics

Typology: and Higher Criticism, 16, 101; methods of, 97–107; traditional, 98–99; Blake's revision of, 98–108; and literary construction, 98n22; as issue in *Jerusalem*, 103. *See also* Christ; Narrative

Tyranny, 1, 3, 137. *See also* Albion; Politics; Saviour; Subject, phenomenalistic; Urizen

Ulro: Sleep of, 70; nature of, 71

"Unformd Memory": and Hume, 115–20

Unitarians, 13–14

Unity, 25, 35; versus multeity, 84

Universal Father, 96

Universality, 36, 91, 106

Univocity: of Bible, 59–61

Urizen: as necessary form of subjectivity, 131

Vala: as effect of narrativity, 124–28; narrative of identity, 126–27; and nature, 128; as Jerusalem's double, 135

Validity, 5, 36, 37, 43, 83

Vision of Albion, 96. *See also* Perception

Vision of the Last Judgment, A. See Blake, works of

Vogler, Thomas, 2, 53n42

Voice: fallen, 74. *See also* Albion; Christ; Epic; Satan; Spectre; Saviour; Vala

Watson, Robert, Lord Bishop of Landaff, 19, 20, 21, 22, 23–24, 99n23, 105. *See also* Authorship; Authenticity; Higher Criticism

Witness, 18. *See also* Belief, conditions of; Rhetoric

Wittreich, Joseph Anthony, Jr., 9n2, 25–26, 27n22

Word, 65. *See also* Blake, his textual practice

Word of God, 36. *See also* Authority; Authenticity; Bible; God; Revelation; Univocity

World, 78–82

Writing, 58. *See also* Barthes, Roland; Citationality; Derrida, Jacques; Textuality

OHIO UNIVERSITY LIBRARY
Please return this book as soon as you have finished with it. In order to avoid a fine it must be returned by the latest date stamped below. All books are subject to recall after two weeks or immediately if needed for reserve.

FEB 2 5 1996

FEB 1 9 1996

CF